Harmonic Practice

BY ROGER SESSIONS

UNIVERSITY OF CALIFORNIA AT BERKELEY

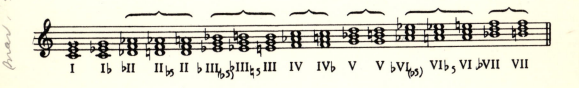

I   Ib   bII   II(b5) II   bIII(b5) bIII(♮5) III   IV   IVb   V   V bVI(b5) VIb5 VI   bVII   VII

HARCOURT, BRACE AND COMPANY   *NEW YORK*

PRINTED IN THE UNITED STATES OF AMERICA

Contents

Foreword

This book had its inception during the years of the Second World War, when the conditions prevailing at Princeton University, where I was then teaching, made it necessary for me to resume charge of the elementary courses — the emergency having claimed both the younger instructors and the older students. The textbooks which I tried out did not quite suit my needs, and I finally replaced them with mimeographed notes of my own. The latter form the basis of the early chapters of this book; they have been revised and expanded, and the later chapters added — all after a considerable interval of time.

When the suggestion was made that the early notes be made the basis of a textbook, I accepted only after considerable misgiving and hesitation. Quite apart from the fact that it meant diverting considerable time away from my primary interests, I found the field already crowded with textbooks on harmony, ranging all the way from theoretical treatises of the first order to less ambitious but quite practical works expressly designed for classroom use. I have, furthermore, always insisted that it is technical mastery and resourcefulness, and not this or that manner of conceiving the so-called "principles," which is finally important; that harmony and counterpoint are, first and last, practical disciplines, and must be always conceived as such; and that theory in the strict sense of the word is essentially without other than pragmatic value.

It was, however, just this consideration which finally convinced me that the project was worth undertaking. Teaching the technique of composition and musical analysis to young composers and others has given me the strong conviction that many of the most problematical aspects of American musical culture can be traced to a confusion of goals in elementary study. It has seemed to me that harmony and counterpoint have often been accepted as desirable studies without sufficiently clear definition of their functions. To some extent this has been the result of traditionalism. It has also been partly due to specific problems which musical education has had to meet in the United States.

As far as traditionalism is concerned, the situation is fairly familiar. The discrepancy between musical theory on the one hand, and the practice of composers on the other, is not a phenomenon of the last twenty or even fifty years; thoughtful musicians have noted it for more than a century, and there has been a steadily increasing number of attempts, by theorists and teachers and even composers, to re-evaluate or reformulate theory in terms more consistent with practice. Meanwhile, except for slight and sporadic changes, the traditional teaching has generally been retained — and retained, far too often, for what seem to be insufficient or obscure reasons. While it is considered a good thing to "study" harmony and counterpoint, and while the disadvantages of neglecting them are widely recognized, the positive aims to be achieved and the goals to be attained are too often simply taken for granted. Since the student is so frequently not clear as to exactly what he is to gain by such study, it is not surprising that he often gains very little.

Some of this confusion, to be sure, is implicit in the prevalent use of the term "theory" to describe the technical training of the composer. The role which musical theory plays in classifying and systematizing technical materials is of course obvious. But, historically considered, it has frequently attempted more than this, and perhaps it has been first of all an effort to formulate immutable artistic principles on the basis of the standards in general acceptance at the time of the formulation. Two facts hardly need to be pointed out: first, that no such "immutable" principles have yet been discovered; secondly, that it has hitherto been precisely the most gifted composers of each generation who have most readily ignored the principles which their immediate predecessors considered as unassailable. This is, in fact, the reason for the discrepancy mentioned above. We are now, however, confronted by the additional fact that even relatively "traditional" composers of today find themselves at variance with the harmony of the textbooks, and that no theory has yet been devised which in a really satisfactory manner covers the field of contemporary music.

At the same time, the rapid growth of the listening public in the United States has tremendously stimulated interest in musical literature and the history of music, and has given rise to a resurgence of interest in musicological studies. It has therefore become easy to justify the traditional teaching of harmony and counterpoint in terms of the "style" of this or that period — generally the sixteenth century in the case of counterpoint, the eighteenth and nineteenth in the case of harmony. This view emphasizes the "style" as such and regards the material studied principally in terms of that style; it tends to regard the solution of the technical problems in these terms, with the successful imitation or the plausible analysis of the music of the period in question as the essential goal of study. It tends to regard what is conceived as "understanding the style" as an end in itself, and as virtually equivalent to the acquisition of harmonic or contrapuntal technique.

I find myself in strong disagreement with this point of view. I too am convinced that the so-called "traditional" materials, both in harmony and counterpoint, must be mastered with the utmost thoroughness, and in respect to harmony I shall try presently to make clear the reasons why I believe this to be so. But I have two general objections to the idea that the study of "style" as such is valid as a point of departure.

First of all, I have observed in the teaching of both harmony and counterpoint that it is quite possible to imitate a "style" very plausibly without possessing any very real technical resourcefulness. The student learns, in other words, to reproduce characteristic formulas and to imitate mannerisms; his efforts are concentrated on reproducing these devices rather than on learning to think, musically, for himself. It is true that a student of composition can sometimes learn a great deal through the minute study of this or that individual work, and through the effort to reproduce the composer's processes of thought as exactly as possible in terms of his own. Such study is, in fact, expressly recommended in this book, in connection with the harmonization of chorales. But, properly conceived, it will emphasize specific technical solutions rather than accurate "stylistic" reproductions, and will perhaps foster the conception of style as consistent musical thought rather than as the conventions of this or that "period" or "school."

Secondly, the idea of a style as a "common practice" is essentially a generalization; it is an artificial concept based largely upon what amounts to statistics, and contains the pitfalls inherent in any statistical approach. It tends to ignore the individual deviations which give music so important a part of its character and vitality, and disregards the fact that the personality of a composer, or even the real nature of an epoch, is to be found as much in what the composer feels free to allow himself, as in his most usual manner of procedure. It would set up a norm or average, and while, as conceived nowadays, it generally does not expressly stigmatize deviations from that norm, it nevertheless leaves them quite out of account. It ignores the fact that deviations too are a vital product of the personality or the milieu which produces them, and even must be reckoned among the most daring flights of imagination of that personality or milieu.

Finally, the evolution of the harmonic idiom has resulted from the fact that musicians of all generations have sought new means of expression, and new syntheses of the means thus discovered. The development of the musical language has been a continuous process. The vital music of any period has roots which reach out in many directions into the past, and shoots which strive in equally manifold fashion into the future. One cannot close this music off and postulate a "common practice" within its boundaries, except by ignoring both the roots and the principle of development which carries it forward.

The pitfall inherent in such a conception consists in

the implication that harmonic thought is static, both within the period and, as it were, at both ends of the period; it treats as a *fait accompli* a process which is actually constantly in the making — as surely in the making during the period between Bach and Brahms as in that between Palestrina and Bach, or between Brahms and the composers of today. Harmony, in other words, is a constant stream of evolution, a constantly changing vocabulary and syntax. We should not allow our sense of the greatness of some of the forms which this evolution has produced to blind us to the fact that their very greatness is dynamic in its nature and its effect; nor should we fall into the all too easy and common error of identifying the highest artistic achievements of a Mozart or a Beethoven with the materials which they utilized, or the conventions which they transcended. If we do this, we teach formulas, however complex; we do not illuminate the processes of musical thought and impulse which at a given point produced the harmonic effects in question, and which finally led beyond these. We furthermore tend — although ultimately without success, and therefore without consequence — to create barriers between tradition and practice instead of revealing and clarifying connections between them. We tend, not to liberate the ear, but rather to bind it and fill it with prejudices.

It seems to me, however, that the goal of harmonic study must be precisely that of liberating the ear, through mastery of resource. The aim is that of enabling the ear to become constantly more aware of, and more sensitive to, the relationships between tones and between aggregates of tones, and constantly more resourceful in making coherent use of these relationships. The student must, in other words, gain such feeling for the materials as can result only from constant, varied, and systematic practice. Whatever classifications, rules, or directions are given him should serve the purpose merely of systematization; they are purely pedagogical in intent, and this strictly utilitarian purpose must be kept before his mind at all points. This seems to me not only the point of departure most appropriate for the training of the composer, but also the soundest basis for the study of "styles." For possibly a style may be most truly understood on the basis of intimacy with musical materials as such, rather than on the basis of an attempt to codify them in terms of general usage.

The above considerations, in any case, have governed the planning of this book. I have tried first of all to present the materials in an order that is logical and easily grasped from the standpoint of the materials themselves, rather than in one based on relative frequency of usage. A good case could, I think, be made for either method, and in adopting the present arrangement I have had in mind the clear and systematic presentation of the materials. I have wanted to provide a framework within which the major problems could be systematically studied in orderly sequence, and in which all available instances could find their places. It is certainly true that such a procedure leaves considerably more to the ear and the initiative of the student than is frequently the case. If this is considered an objection, my answer is that I have always found the principle a pedagogically sound one. One learns chiefly by experience, very seldom by precept.

The problem is, then, to provide the student with the opportunity for abundant experience, and to encourage him, on the basis of this experience, to trust himself. I believe I have learned that students — the average as well as the exceptional — respond most readily when confronted with real challenges, and that, in a general way, even unsuccessful efforts to meet such challenges are incomparably more productive of worth-while results than the relatively easy fulfillment of carefully graded tasks.

The experience of nearly twenty years in teaching composition has left me more than ever convinced of the necessity of thorough mastery of what used to be known as the "fundamentals" and what today is frequently called "traditional harmony." This mastery is necessary, however, not because the material in question is "traditional," but because it is *primary*. The sense of harmonic contrast, of the rhythmic effect inherent in harmonic progression, and of tonal structure, can be effectively developed only on the basis of a feeling for the simplest materials — the so-called "consonant chords"; there is no misconception more dangerous to a student's development than the still all too widely held assumption that it is "practical" to neglect the study of these materials, or to cut it short. In like manner, the relation of the "vertical" to the "horizontal" elements in music can be adequately grasped only as a result of a thoroughly developed sense for the more elementary forms and uses of dissonance; and this latter implies at least some experience in the stricter usages — even though these have long since been superseded by others which have, as it were, evolved out of them. Above all I have found it to be true that a thorough grounding in the fundamentals is by far the most efficient means through which a student can gain an insight into the all-important subject of articulation. As I have tried to indicate (pp. 402–404), the problem of the cadence can scarcely be solved, today, in the older terms; but I am convinced at the same time that it is rarely solved at all unless the student has acquired a real mastery of those terms and a real resourcefulness in using them.

The term "tonicization" is an Anglicized form of the German "*Tonikalisierung*," coined, I believe, by Heinrich Schenker. Though I am far from subscribing to all of Schenker's theories, this conception seems to me of the greatest value, not only for the analysis of musical form, but for the clarification of the nature of harmonic thinking and especially of harmonic elaboration. In a more practical sense I have found it less cumbersome to adopt, in this instance, an inclusive term which designates a familiar process of harmonic thought — a process which is actually much broader in scope than the one covered by the theory of secondary dominants. If the distinction between tonicization and modulation is clearly understood in principle, it is quite unnecessary to labor the frequent instances which may be regarded as either the one or the other, the answer depending upon whether the instance is regarded in its relation to detail or to larger structure. I have interpreted the term in the way that seemed to me to be most appropriate, without attempting to determine how far my definition coincided exactly with Schenker's.

In the final chapters I have attempted to show some

of the lines of continuity between the traditional harmonic ideas and some of the aspects of present-day harmonic practice. My aim here has been above all a practical one, as indeed it has been throughout the book. It is these chapters above all that may be considered controversial, largely because, as I have indicated (pp. 333 ff., 344, 393 ff.), the development of chromatic harmony has, in my opinion, brought about situations in which the concept of root progression is no longer sufficient. My endeavor has always been to keep clearly in mind a distinction between the strictly harmonic or "vertical" impulse, which arises from a clearly felt relationship between chord roots (or, if you will, harmonies in their functional sense), and the linear or "horizontal" impulse, which arises from the movement and design of voices. If the concept of root progression is to be valid, in other words, it must be felt and heard as an essential musical fact, and not remain as merely a theoretical convenience. Actually, I do not feel that vertical relationships of this type are wholly absent from any of the contemporary music which I know and value; I find that they always play an important role in large structure, though very often they exist in forms which defy exact analysis in accordance with any terms which we have at hand. But I find also that it is of dubious value to seek root relationships in contexts (as, for instance, of the type illustrated on pp. 342–343) where the impulse and the logic are clearly linear in origin and character. The concepts of root and root progression rest primarily on relationships of quite another sort; and in view of the close and essential connection between root relationship and movement (see especially pp. 77–92,

200 ff., etc.) it seems to me both relevant and useful to lay considerable stress on the distinction between what is "horizontal" or linear, and what is "vertical" or harmonic.

Any analytical concept, however, is almost of necessity an oversimplification, and I would be the last to deny that even the most uncompromisingly "horizontal" context has also its "vertical" aspect, just as the converse is also true. For this reason I feel impelled to warn the reader once more that this book is intended as essentially a practical handbook of harmonic materials, and in no sense as a treatise on harmonic theory. Nothing interests me less than dogmatism in questions of musical theory — it is the most arid form of dogmatism that I can well conceive, and the least in accord with the realities of the situation which it pretends to interpret. The ear of the musician, as used both in creating and in apprehending, must remain the court of last appeal; and musical theory thus remains, at the very best, a more or less adequate descriptive account of the ear's experiences. In my opinion it is chimerical to demand that musical theory should, or to hope that it could, be more than that.

The effective core of this book, then, is in the exercises, since it is from these that the student will really learn. I have tried to provide him with a text which consists of general indications rather than prescriptions, and to make the illustrations as simple and as clear as possible. Very few of the illustrations are taken, as is so generally the custom, from actual works; I have tried instead to provide abundant references indicating where such quotations can be found. My reasons for doing this are twofold. First of all, I have wished to illustrate each point in as simple terms as possible, using the general type of four-voiced chordal harmony which the student himself will first be using. I have often found that the student is confused if he is confronted with examples of a more complex type before he has thoroughly studied the materials in the form which he can most easily grasp. Secondly, I have found that the usefulness of such quotations is seriously impaired by the fact that they are necessarily limited to a few measures taken out of context. In many — perhaps most — cases this involves a real distortion of the musical sense. Such a quotation rarely presents a complete rhythmic unit, and sometimes perforce omits that part of the phrase which is necessary if the real significance, rhythmic or otherwise, of the point in question is to be made clear. I have tried to make my references definite, abundant, and accessible, and have given considerable thought to their choice.

In planning the exercises I have been much and obviously influenced by the admirable but little-known handbook of Iwan Knorr, *Aufgaben für den Unterricht in der Harmonielehre* (Breitkopf & Härtel, 1894), the qualities of which I learned to appreciate as a student, and later as a teacher. The same principles are applied with some modification in Paul Hindemith's *Traditional Harmony*, to which this book also owes something. The student will generally find exercises in which prescribed harmonies are presented in various aspects: figures alone; figured basses; and melodies either with harmonies indicated or, later, with a given bass. For these exercises the student is expected to find the most musically satisfying solutions of which he is capable; they are designed both to help him to attain, through varied practice, dexterity in handling the mechanics of four-voiced harmony, and to serve as models for the treatment of the exercises which follow, in which the student must provide his own harmonies. In each group of exercises I have tried to proceed from the relatively simple to the more complex. My aim has been to provide a number of exercises sufficient to meet all possible needs. The number of exercises actually worked by the student will depend, of course, on a number of factors for which exact provision cannot be made in a textbook. I consider it important, however, that the student should work at least a few exercises of each type, in order to attain the greater resourcefulness which results from approaching each problem from several different directions.

I have, furthermore, tried to confront the student with technical problems sufficiently exacting to bring into play whatever ingenuity he has at his disposal, and to enable him to meet with confidence such technical situations as will inevitably confront him when he attempts to compose on his own. I make no apology, therefore, for the fact that the exercises are frequently difficult. My experience in using many of them has shown me that exercises of this type hold the student's interest even when his solutions are far from perfect — that by demanding more rather than less of him, they really cultivate his powers to the utmost. He will find, I think, that even the comparatively unsuccessful solution of a later group of exercises will still help to make possible the successful solution of earlier ones, and that his technical proficiency will grow the faster for this method. The point of an exercise is, to state it once more, not so much the perfect solution, as the experience and the proficiency gained through grappling with the problems involved.

Finally, the exercises may and should be frequently supplemented by efforts at making original use of the materials studied. I have made no provision for this in the text, since it seems to me a matter best left to the individual teacher or student. But it should never be forgotten that the ultimate criterion of harmonic study is the ability of the student to think for himself in harmonic terms, and it is precisely this ability that nothing but actual composition, on however small a scale, can effectively furnish.

ROGER SESSIONS

Berkeley, California
January, 1951

Acknowledgments

Any book of this nature owes a great deal to a great many people. I have already mentioned my indebtedness to the writings of Paul Hindemith and of Heinrich Schenker, an indebtedness which I feel no less keenly for the fact that I have found myself frequently in disagreement with each of them. I have also indicated my debt to Iwan Knorr, the teacher of my teacher, Ernest Bloch. I owe the greatest personal debt, of course, to the latter, who in fact — and from quite literally the first ten minutes of my study with him — showed me the beginnings of the path along which my thoughts and my impulses in respect to harmony were to travel in the thirty-one years that have followed. I owe a debt of another kind, of course, to Arnold Schönberg, to whom the whole epoch which coincides with my own musical experience and career owes so incalculably much. It becomes always clearer that the influence of this truly extraordinary man is not limited to his most immediate or obvious followers, but has had a far-reaching effect on friend and foe alike. His *Harmonielehre*, many later writings, and above all his music, have set in motion trains of thought, as they have opened new avenues of musical sensibility, of human awareness — in a word, of musical experience — which are at the very least a challenge to all musicians of today.

More specifically, I owe very warm thanks: to Mrs. Katherine M. Bryan of Princeton, who helped me in preparing the original notes from which the book grew; to my wife, who did the same for the book itself; to my

California colleagues, Professors Manfred Bukofzer, William Denny, Albert Elkus, Joaquin Nin-Culmell, and Messrs. Andrew Imbrie and Edgar Sparks; and to Professor Edward Cone and Mr. Milton Babbitt of Princeton, and Mr. Walter Nollner of Williams College — all of whom helped me most generously with advice and criticism, with the fruitful exchange of ideas, and with observations of a pedagogical nature which have helped me immeasurably in giving the book its final form. My pupils Miss Jeanne Shapiro and Mr. Robert Helps also have been of great assistance — the latter in preparing the manuscript. Professor Marion Bauer of New York University, and my former pupil Mr. Christopher Reid, have performed valiant service in editing the book for the printer.

R. S.

Introductory Remarks

Harmony, in the technical sense, may be defined as that aspect of music which has to do with chords and the relationships between them; or in more complex terms, with the effects produced —

1. By tones sounded, or apprehended by the ear, simultaneously — as in a chord; or in close harmonic association — as, for instance, in an arpeggio, a scale, or a more complex group of tones, melodic or otherwise, in which harmonic intervals are stressed in such a way as to produce a harmonic effect.

2. By the progressions from one such harmonic unit to another.

3. By the larger patterns and structures which can be formed from such progressions, in combination with, and to some degree subordinate to, the other aspects of music — melody and rhythm.

From the definitions above, it follows that the student of harmony is to study, through practice, how to construct chords, how to connect chords, and how to use chords for the purposes of musical expression and design.

His aim will be twofold: first, to gain the sharpest possible awareness of the nature and effect of the materials he is using; secondly, to gain an ever wider experience of the resources at his disposal, with the ultimate goal, if he is a composer, of mastering these resources and bending them to the uses of his musical conception.

It should be clearly understood from the beginning, therefore, that the study of harmony is not primarily training in *writing*, but training in hearing; that the student's first preoccupation must be to grasp harmonic facts and effects through the use of his ear. As long as he needs the help of an instrument for this purpose, he must avail himself of it to the extent necessary. He should, however, make every effort to develop his ability to "hear" inwardly — an ability which everyone possesses to some degree unless physically handicapped. In any case, it is essential for him to cultivate the habit of not writing a note unless he is sure of its sound, and to develop the accuracy and refinement of his musical hearing through incessant practice.

On any other basis the study of harmony is literally meaningless, and therefore a waste of time.

CHAPTER

ONE

Relationships between Tones

1. THE OVERTONE SERIES

A useful point of departure for the study of harmony may be found in the first six "partial tones" of the overtone series, a natural acoustical phenomenon.

Musical tones are produced by the regular vibration of "sonorous bodies"; in most cases these latter are either columns of air, as in the case of the voice or the wind instruments, or taut strings, as in the case of the various types of stringed instrument. The detailed facts regarding the production of musical tone may be learned from any reference book on acoustical physics, and need not detain us here. The immediately relevant fact is that the vibration of a sonorous body produces, nearly always, not a single tone, but a whole complex of simultaneous tones called "*partials*."

There are partial tones because the sonorous body vibrates in a very complex manner — not only as a whole, but also, and simultaneously, in all of its fractions. Presumably every equal division ($\frac{1}{2}$, $\frac{1}{3}$, $\frac{1}{4}$, etc.) vibrates and produces at least a theoretical tone; and these tones contribute to the total effect of each musical sound.

The following table shows the twelve lowest partial tones of C, on the basis of the "open" C-string of the violoncello. Since it is only the relationships of the partial tones which are important for our present purpose, the

FIG. 1

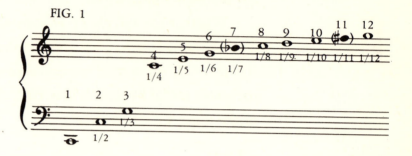

numbers in the upper row represent, not the number of vibrations per second [1] but the relation between the vibration frequencies of the various partials. The fractions in the lower row give the fractions of the whole sonorous body which produce the respective partial tones, and hence also the relative lengths of the sonorous bodies which produce the tones in question.

According to a different terminology, the first partial is called the "*fundamental*" tone; the upper partials, beginning with the second, are called "*overtones.*" Thus the second partial is the first overtone, the third partial is the second overtone, etc.

It will be noted that the lower partials are strengthened by the fact that not only are they produced by larger segments of the whole, but they are also duplicated in each successive higher octave. Thus, in the series illustrated in Figure 1, the tone C occurs four times, the tone

[1] The reader who is curious in this regard may multiply the figures in the upper row by 65.25. He should remember, however, that this is only one of a number of tunings which are in fairly general use.

G three times, the tone E twice. It should also be noted that the seventh and the eleventh partials are not pitched exactly on B-flat and F-sharp, but are lower, toward A and F; they are therefore tones which, in our system, are definitely out of tune.

Whether for the above reasons or not, it is to the first six partial tones that the simplest of three-toned chords — *the major triad* — may be compared. The comparison is useful because it illustrates clearly the relation of the tones within the triad.

2. SCALES AND KEYS

The first six partials (shown at the left) may, by eliminating duplications, be reduced to the C major triad .

The interval of a fifth

Of fundamental importance is the interval of a *fifth* formed by the second (hence also the first) partial (C in the above examples) and the third partial (G in the above examples). Any two tones which lie a fifth apart may be considered to be in the closest possible harmonic relationship; much will be noted later in regard to the very far-reaching importance of this fact.

The tone C is therefore closely related, not only to G, its third partial, but to F, of which C in turn constitutes the third partial.

Since the lower partials are readily apprehended by the ear, and can therefore be considered as a part of general and demonstrable experience, a very good case may be made for the above explanation, which implies a causal connection between the overtone series and the elementary facts of harmony. The writer is firmly convinced, however, that it is not the physical facts themselves, but our experience of these facts, which has brought about this connection. Musicians have always used whatever materials they have found ready at hand and capable of utilization, and it is the musical imagination of composers that has molded these materials and given them significant character. It is therefore the musical ear, not the physical nature of sound, which must be regarded as the final point of reference; and the explanation of the one in terms of the other remains so purely conjectural, even dubious, as to be, at best, misleading.

Admittedly, the ear is a far more difficult point of reference, for the musical theorist, than the physical nature of sound; for the "musical ear" — by which is meant the sum of all the faculties, psychological as well as physiological, which enter into our apprehension of music — is highly complex, influenced by all kinds of cultural and individual nuances, and hence difficult to describe with precision. This, however, makes it not less but more important to insist upon the fact that acoustical physics and music are in quite different categories, and that though there are apparent points of contact between them, the two fields should be clearly differentiated in musical speculation and analysis. The overtone series has been used to "prove" many differing theories and to reinforce many differing sets of values. These proofs and evaluations, however, cannot be derived from the overtone series; they must instead be sought in terms of the various types of satisfaction which the ear — i.e., the musical imagination — demands and receives from music.

In the opinion of the writer, then, the significance of the overtone series for purposes of harmonic study cannot be carried any further than is indicated above.

The diatonic scale

If now we construct a major triad on G 𝄞 we acquire two tones, B and D, which we may add to those found already in the major triad of C. In similar fashion, the major triad of F 𝄞 furnishes us with two additional tones, F and A.

By adding all of these tones together within the range of a single octave, we have the tones of the *C major diatonic scale*. This scale is shown below, with the tones of which it is composed, and also with Roman numerals representing the *degrees of the scale*.

FIG. 2

Tones:	C	D	E	F	G	A	B	(C)
Degrees of the Scale:	I	II	III	IV	V	VI	VII	(I)

While the tones describe only the *C major* diatonic scale, the degrees in Roman numerals are used in referring to *any* diatonic scale.

There are seven degrees of the scale in each octave. The degrees of the scale and the chords constructed upon them (see p. 31), are not only numbered, but have also been given names, of which the sense will appear more clearly as the relations between the various degrees within the key are more fully understood.

I, the "key tone," is called the *"tonic."* Its upper fifth, V, is called the *"dominant."* Its lower fifth, IV, is called the *"subdominant."*

Halfway between tonic and dominant, ascending, lies III, which is called the *"mediant"*; halfway between tonic and subdominant, descending, lies VI, known as the *"submediant."*

VII, because of its tendency to move up a half step

to the tonic, is called the "*leading tone*." The French term for the same tone — "*la note sensible*," which may be translated as "the sensitive tone" — describes this tendency even more vividly.

II is generally, and illogically, called the "*supertonic*," by false analogy with "subdominant." This latter term is actually an ambiguous translation of the Italian "*sottodominante*" or German "*Unterdominante*," literally "lower dominant" — i.e. the lower fifth as distinguished from the dominant or upper fifth. "Subdominant" does not mean "the tone just below the dominant."

Figure 3, below, shows graphically the relationships of the various degrees of the scale to I, the tonic.

FIG. 3

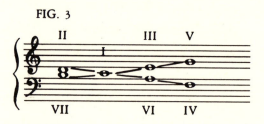

The circle of fifths

We can, of course, form other triads, by proceeding upward by fifths from G and downward by fifths from F. By this means we add several new tones to those of the diatonic scale. The upper fifths give us F♯ and C♯; the lower fifths give us B♭, E♭, A♭, D♭, G♭, and C♭ (Fig. 4).

FIG. 4

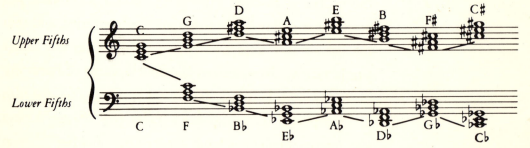

Arranging our fifths in the form of a circle, we get the following picture:

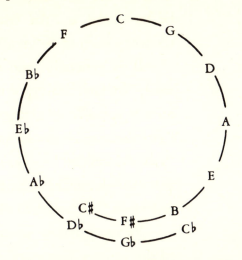

This is known in musical theory as the *"circle of fifths,"* and the student will find it a convenience from several points of view. If, however, we check it in terms of the overtone series we find that in fact it is not a circle, since the B and C-flat, the F-sharp and G-flat, and the C-sharp and D-flat, as obtained in this manner, are not exactly equal in pitch, the flats in each case being lower than the corresponding sharps. The general subject of "temperament" or tuning is very complex and there is no need to go into it here. For present purposes it is sufficient to recall that the "tempered" scale, according to which the octave is divided into twelve equal semitones, has been in general use for more than two centuries, and that the use of this scale has, perhaps more than any other single factor, characterized the development of harmony in that period. It remains none the less true that the fifth as "tempered" is somewhat smaller (or "flatter"), and the major third somewhat larger (or "sharper"), than the corresponding intervals produced respectively by the third and the fifth partials; and that the tempered D-flat and C-sharp differ from each other in sense and function, if not in pitch. (Also, string players, and others whose instruments allow such differentiations as between D-flat and C-sharp, frequently make these minute differentiations in performance, in the interests of a purer intonation.)

It is customary to regard sharps as belonging in general to the ascending chromatic scale, and flats as belonging to the descending chromatic scale:

FIG. 5

This is a generalization which will be much modified by the later study of harmony; it is, however, useful as a provisional working principle.

Definition of "key"

The relationships which led us (pp. 7–8) to the construction of the diatonic scale of C major form the basis also of what is called the "key" of C major. A "*key*," in this sense of the word, is a set of relationships between tones, established in such a way that one tone — the *tonic* — becomes predominant, as the center to which the ear relates all of the other relationships, and as the conclusive tone toward which, in effect, they all tend. It is the composer who, through his musical conception, sets up these relationships in such a manner that the ear of the listener grasps them clearly. A very important phase of the study of harmony has to do, either directly or by implication, with the manner in which a key is "*established*"; or, in other words, the means by which the listener is induced to orient his sensations toward a given tonic.

3. INTERVALS

The expression "relationships between tones" will perhaps be better understood at this point in terms of the basic relationships which are called "*intervals.*" An interval may be described as the relationship between two tones sounded simultaneously or in succession. The term "relationship," as used in this connection, must be understood, *as must every term used in this book*, to describe something actually heard — a definite *musical sensation*, with which the student must learn to familiarize himself thoroughly. *He should, in fact, strive constantly to associate musical terms with actual sounds — or, to be more precise, accurately remembered sensations — rather than with abstract ideas.*

Major, minor, and perfect intervals

Intervals are called "*seconds,*" "*thirds,*" etc., according to the number of degrees (p. 7) which one can count from either note to the other, including the note from which one starts. The "*prime*" or "*unison,*" which indicates the simultaneous sounding — for example, by two or more voices or instruments — of the same tone, is also classed among the intervals, even though there is obviously no "interval" between the notes.

Figure 6 shows the intervals formed (a) above and (b) below the tonic by the various degrees of the C major scale.

FIG. 6 *(a)*

(b)

Intervals larger than an octave are known as *"compound intervals,"* and may be named either according to their actual size (tenth, eleventh, etc.) or by the names of the simpler intervals to which they merely add one or more octaves. Thus ♪ may be called either a twelfth or a fifth, depending on the given context.

If we measure the intervals by semitones we will see immediately certain differences between (a) and (b) in Figure 6. The seconds, thirds, sixths, and sevenths in (a) are larger, each by one semitone, than those in (b) (while the fourths and fifths — and, of course, the octaves — are of the same size in both). The two forms, larger and smaller, of seconds, thirds, sixths, and sevenths in the diatonic scale are called *"major"* and *"minor."* As these intervals occur in (a) they are major; in (b) they are minor. The terms "major" and "minor" were originally applied, in fact, to intervals; their use in connection with the major and minor triads and modes was derived from this, as will be seen later.

The fourths, fifths, and octaves in Figure 6 are called *"perfect"* intervals.

Since the intervals in (a) contain the same tones as those in (b), we may also note another group of facts. Two intervals containing the same tones, but in inverse order (the lower tone of the one being the higher tone of the other), are called *"inversions"* with respect to each other. Thus a second is the inversion of a seventh, a third of a sixth, a fourth of a fifth, and vice versa. Also, the inversion of a major interval is always a minor interval, while the inversion of a perfect interval is another perfect interval.

Augmented and diminished intervals

One more interval may be found among the tones of the diatonic scale. The fourth and seventh degrees of the scale — the notes F and B — form an interval of six semitones. This is a semitone larger than a perfect fourth, and is called an *"augmented"* fourth. Its inversion, composed of the notes B and F, is called the *"diminished"* fifth, and is one semitone smaller than a perfect fifth. The diminished fifth also contains six semitones, and thus is identical in sound, though not in sense, with the augmented fourth.

This interval, which divides the octave in half, belongs for this reason in a quite special category, and — because it is composed of three whole tones (six semitones) — is often called the *"tritone,"* a term which is convenient since it applies to both inversions. The sense of the two inversions differs within any given harmonic context; but in the absence of such a context the effect is ambiguous. For example, the interval comprises the seventh and fourth degrees of A major (see Fig. 17), but the same tones, written or, as is sometimes said, "spelled" differently, constitute the fourth and seventh degrees of E-flat major.

The augmented fifth ♯ is, of course, one semitone larger than the perfect fifth; the diminished fourth ♯ is one semitone smaller than the perfect fourth. Augmented seconds, thirds, sixths, and sevenths are each one semitone larger than the respective major intervals:

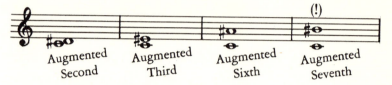

Augmented Second   Augmented Third   Augmented Sixth   Augmented Seventh

while diminished seconds, thirds, etc., are one semitone smaller than the like-named minor intervals.

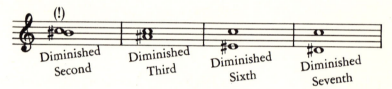

Diminished Second   Diminished Third   Diminished Sixth   Diminished Seventh

Consonance and dissonance

Intervals are traditionally classified as *"consonant"* or *"dissonant."* The definition of these terms has been very frequently confused by the tendency to associate the idea of "consonance" with the idea of sounds that are "pleasing," "satisfying," or "harmonious," "dissonant" being thus taken to describe sounds that are essentially "disagreeable," "harsh," or "incoherent." Actually, "consonant" and "dissonant" are precise technical terms, and have nothing to do with the "sweetness" or "harshness" of the sounds in question. Effects so described depend on many factors, some of them obviously subjective, and have no necessary connection with the relationships of the tones involved — these remain consonant or dissonant regardless of how the hearer feels about them.

Like many musical terms, consonance and dissonance are extremely hard to define as principles. Any definition that is at all adequate will allow for the idea that consonances are static and conclusive, dissonances dynamic and inconclusive. The definition may contain also the idea of what has been called "fusion" — consonances being intervals in which the two tones involved seem to "fuse" together and be heard as a single unit of sound, while dissonances are heard primarily as separate tones, ready to move their separate ways. The trouble with such definitions is that they are not only purely relative, but also lean heavily on the individual listener, and that listeners — even very good ones — differ widely in the manner in which they interpret musical sensations of this kind.

Three types of consonance

Perhaps it is better, therefore, to define consonant intervals as simple relationships between tones, dissonances as more complex relationships. (It is of course not the definition, but familiarity with the facts, that is important.) The "consonant" intervals are those which are found within the triad, or, in other terms, the relationships which can be found among the first six partial tones (Fig. 1), and the inversions of these intervals, namely —

1. Intervals based on the fundamental:
Perfect octave (1st and 2d partials)
Perfect fifth (2d and 3d   "   )
Major third   (4th and 5th "   )
2. Inversions of the above:
Perfect fourth (3d and 4th partials)
Minor sixth   (5th and 8th   "   )

3. Intervals formed by overtones other than the upper octaves of the fundamental:

Minor third (5th and 6th partials)

Major sixth (3d and 5th   "   )

It will be readily noted that the perfect consonances differ in character from the thirds and sixths — the degree of "fusion" being greater in the perfect consonances. It may be noted further that the perfect fourth is treated, under certain harmonic circumstances, as a dissonance (see Chapter Six), and that in strict counterpoint it is also generally classified among the dissonances. This is due principally to the fact that it is the inversion of the all-important interval of a fifth, and the effect of the fourth is to emphasize in the most drastic fashion the fact of inversion as such. The fundamental is here the upper, not the lower tone, and largely for this reason the interval seems "incomplete."

Three types of dissonance

Dissonances may be classified in three general types: seconds and sevenths (both major and minor); tritones; and the other augmented and diminished intervals.

Seconds and sevenths, furthermore, differ in that the former are composed of tones which lie on successive degrees of the scale. When the tones in question are sounded successively, in other words, seconds have in general no *harmonic* implication, as do the other intervals; one is hardly aware of the relationship between the tones, but rather of the movement from one tone to the next above or below. On the other hand, when the tones of a second are sounded together, the specifically "dissonant" quality is found in what may be considered its purest form; that is, the two tones seem to contain within themselves the impulse to move to other tones, but if seconds are played by themselves — that is, out of context — they do not imply a specific harmony. Sevenths, on the other hand, "include" consonant intervals; in listening to them we very readily supply these intervals in imagination, giving the interval the sense of an incomplete chord — thus: ?

We do not invariably do this, however, and one of the pitfalls of harmonic analysis consists in basing one's deductions on tones which are not present in the music, but which, according to this or that theory, may be postulated. The above remarks on sevenths should therefore be taken in the most general sense, as a means of aiding the student to become more aware of actual differences in sound and in effect. It must be emphasized over and over again that it is always the concrete musical context that finally matters, not the character of an interval or chord taken in isolation. It is not the individual chord, interval, or tone which constitutes music, but the whole pattern of sound, or, more accurately, the pattern of movement in sound — and the sense of that pattern of movement.

In regard to seconds and sevenths, it may also be observed that the minor second and the major seventh are "sharper" dissonances than the major second and the minor seventh.

The tritone has already been discussed in detail (pp. 13–14). Its characteristic ambiguity places it in a special category, and has given it a quite special role in the development of harmony. The student will be readily aware of the tendency of the augmented fourth to expand [musical notation] and of the diminished fifth to contract [musical notation] . He will also be able to observe that if, in the above examples, we change the F to E♯, we obtain the opposite results: [musical notation]

It is, of course, the musical context which will determine whether, in any given case, the tritone will be heard as an augmented fourth or as a diminished fifth. If the tritone is heard out of context, the tendency will be to supply one — that is, to hear the interval as definitely one of its two forms — but observers will be likely to disagree in any given case until the context is supplied.

The third type of dissonance includes the remaining augmented and diminished intervals: seconds, thirds, sixths, sevenths, and octaves; the diminished fourth and the augmented fifth; and the chromatic interval formed by two tones which lie on the same degree but which differ in pitch.

In order to understand the third type of dissonance it is necessary to have some knowledge of what is known as "*enharmonic change*." This term denotes the principle which underlies the difference between two notes which are written differently though, in the "tempered" system of tuning, they are similar in pitch: the difference, say, between C♯ and D♭, or between F and E♯. For the moment, the remarks on pages 9–10, with reference to the chromatic scale, will suffice for a preliminary understanding of enharmonic change; but the student should take careful note of those which will follow presently in regard to the various keys and the principles which govern their notation, and apply these principles in later situations involving enharmonic change.

The point here is that the intervals of the third type of dissonance all correspond in pitch, though not in sense, to intervals already studied. Figure 7 should make this clear:

FIG. 7 (a)

As far as pitch is concerned, (a) and (b), and (c) and (d), in Figure 7, are identical; but the minor intervals in (a) have, through enharmonic change, become augmented intervals in (b), while the major intervals in (c) have been enharmonically changed to diminished intervals in (d).

It will be noticed, however, that, since all four sections of Figure 7 picture the chromatic scale in the ascending order, it is (b) and (d) which are, in this case, correctly written. In like manner, (a) and (c) would be correct if the intervals were written in descending order. In other words, an augmented interval — as, indeed, the name implies — must be conceived as the enlargement by a semitone of a major or perfect interval; and a diminished interval as the diminution by a semitone of a minor or perfect interval. Needless to say, it may be the alteration of either the higher or the lower tone of the interval which produces the augmentation or the diminution.

The following are further examples of augmented and diminished intervals.

FIG. 8

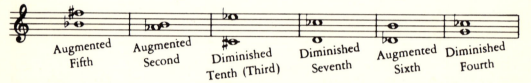

Augmented Fifth · Augmented Second · Diminished Tenth (Third) · Diminished Seventh · Augmented Sixth · Diminished Fourth

The intervals of the third type of dissonance derive a part, and in some cases the whole, of their dissonant character from the musical context in which they appear. They are dissonant precisely because their relationship in the given context is complex rather than simple; but they are not the less dissonant on that account. This is a very important fact, which emphasizes the point that consonance and dissonance are terms which have to do with the musical sense of intervals, not with the data of acoustical physics, except in the cases where these data can be shown to have a direct bearing on the musical facts in question. This is of course only another way of saying that the musical sense is decisive in any case.

Summary of the intervals

Figure 9 summarizes all of the intervals. It cannot be too strongly emphasized that the ability to recognize these intervals readily by ear is an absolute necessity for the student of harmony, and that he should make the achievement of this ability his first concentrated effort.

FIG. 9

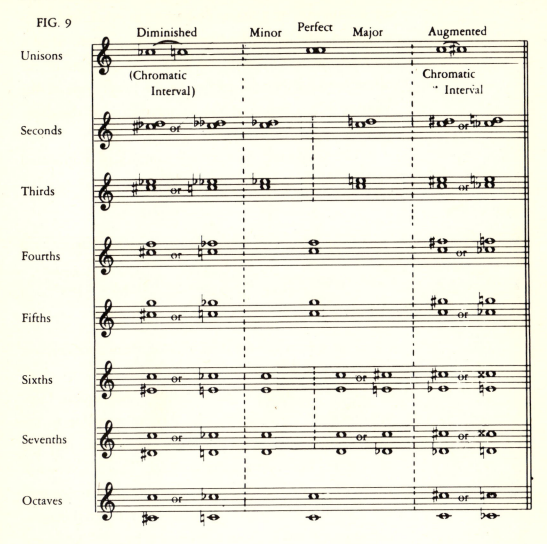

4. THE MAJOR AND MINOR MODES

Diatonic major scales and key signatures

The student will now be able to construct the major scale on any tone. Two points must be kept clearly in mind. First of all, the major (also the minor) scale is always *diatonic:* this means simply that there will be one tone, and only one, on each degree. Secondly, it need hardly be said that the relationships will be the same in every major scale. Beginning with the tonic, the second and third degrees will follow, each a major second higher than the tone preceding; the fourth will follow at the interval of a minor second higher than the third; the fifth, sixth, and seventh are each a major second higher than the tone preceding. The upper octave of the tonic will thus be a minor second higher than the seventh degree, or leading tone. We show by way of example the intervals of the C major scale:

FIG. 10

also, the E major scale:

FIG. 11

and the scale of D-flat major:

FIG. 12

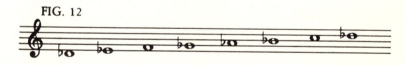

The sharps or flats which occur in the various scales are generally — not always — indicated at the beginning of a piece or a passage in a given key, by what is known as the *"key signature."* This device relieves the composer of the necessity of repeating sharp or flat signs before each note to which they apply, and helps the reader of the music to grasp more clearly the tonal relationships within the piece or passage in question.

At this point the circle of fifths (p. 9) becomes very useful. It indicates not only the order of the keys but also the order in which sharps or flats are added to the various signatures. The sharps, beginning with F♯ in the key of G major, are added in the following order, proceeding clockwise around the circle: F♯, C♯, G♯, D♯, A♯, E♯, and B♯; the flats, beginning with B♭ in the key of F major, and proceeding counterclockwise: B♭, E♭, A♭, D♭, G♭, C♭, and F♭.

The following table, which gives the signatures of the major keys, should make this clear:

FIG. 13

Key and mode   Each key has two forms — the so-called major and minor *modes*. The distinction between *keys* and *modes* should be clearly kept in mind: the term "key" defines the *locality* of the tonic, and therefore of the dominant, subdominant, and other degrees within the scale; while the "mode" defines the *character* of the relationships within the scale, in terms of the intervals between degrees. Thus we speak of the *key* of C or A or F♯, but of the major or minor *mode*. The key of C, or any other key, may be either major or minor, and, as will be seen in Chapter Ten, changes of mode, especially in the music of the last two hundred years, very often take place rapidly and freely within a given passage.

**Minor scales and
key signatures**

In the minor mode the primary relationships of tonic, dominant, and subdominant remain the same as in the major mode. In the so-called "pure" minor scale, the third, the sixth, and the seventh degrees are minor intervals with respect to the tonic:

FIG. 14

The minor seconds occur, in this scale, between the second and third, and between the fifth and sixth, degrees. As will be seen later, the minor mode is more complex in treatment than the major mode, and the "pure" minor scale must be considered as only a point of departure. But it is from this "pure" scale that the minor signatures are derived, as follows:

FIG. 15

The degrees are named as in the major mode, with the exception of the seventh degree which is not properly a "leading tone" in the form which occurs in the "pure" minor scale. In order to function as a leading tone, the seventh degree must be chromatically raised a semitone, in order to bring it closer to the tonic, and thus to obtain the effect of "attraction" toward the tonic which gives the "leading tone" its name and character. This alteration occurs extremely often, but is never indicated in the key signature; it is always indicated by an "accidental" sharp, double sharp (see p. 28), or natural, e.g.:

FIG. 16

It is customary to indicate major intervals, scales, and keys with capital letters; minor intervals, scales, and keys with small letters. Thus "the key of G" means G major; "g" means g minor. "M.6" is a major sixth; "m.6" is a minor sixth, etc.

Relationships of major and minor keys

It will be noted that each key signature of a minor scale is identical with that of one of the major scales: C major with a minor, G major with e minor, etc. The student should not let himself be confused by this fact, or by the fact that the keys thus associated are called "relative" major and minor keys. The "relationship" indicated by this term is a real one, in that the scales contain the same tones; also, the inexperienced composer can easily slip unawares from a minor key into its relative major or, less frequently, from a major key into its relative minor. Further, the mediant (here the relative major) relationship is considerably more important in the minor mode than in the major mode. But the student should learn to associate, above all, the two modes as they are built on the same tonic: C major and c minor, F major and f minor, etc. These keys are, despite the difference in signature, identical in a very real sense, and a well-developed ear will recognize that in passing from the one to the other there is no *movement*, but simply a change of color or character. Composers have treated this fact as a fundamental premise of key relationship ever since the sense of key became strongly developed; and an understanding of this fact and of all of its implications is quite essential to the understanding of the musical language of the past three hundred years. The following table, therefore, should be studied carefully.

FIG. 17

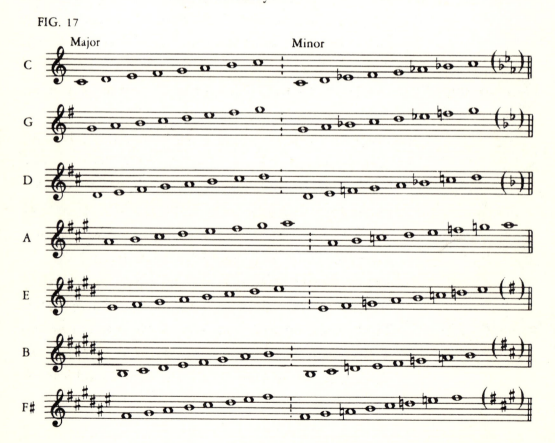

The chromatic scale

Finally, it should be observed that, while the diatonic scale — major or minor — may be regarded as a kind of schematic summary indicating the principal relationships within a key, the tones outside the diatonic scale are also essentially within the key, although forming only subordinate relationships. Because of these relationships, the chromatic scale has a somewhat different written form in each of the various keys, and the principle illustrated in Figure 5 (see p. 10) should be reapplied to each key, the diatonic steps being altered similarly, each in turn, as the scale rises or falls.

For instance, this is the chromatic scale of E-flat major:

FIG. 18

and this is the chromatic scale of c-sharp minor:

FIG. 19

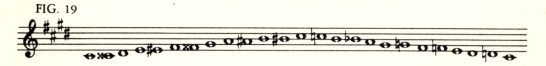

Figures 18 and 19 demonstrate the basic function of the double sharp (𝄪) and double flat (♭♭). In practice, these symbols are used somewhat less consistently than the strictest logic would demand; e.g., in the descending chromatic scale of E♭ (Fig. 18), A♮ would nearly always be used in preference to B♭♭. The student, however, will find it most useful to be conservative, at first, in this regard; once he has acquired a real feeling for the logic and the subtleties of musical sense and musical notation, he can — and certainly should! — eschew pedantry in this as in all other respects, and adopt the simplest notation which is compatible with the clear expression of his musical ideas.

5. TONALITY

The whole system of relationships between tones, which is embodied in the twelve major keys, the twelve minor keys, and the relationships between the various harmonies and the various keys, is called the tonal system, or "*tonality*." Tonality should be understood as the principal means which the composers of the seventeenth, eighteenth, and nineteenth centuries evolved of organizing musical sounds and giving them coherent shape. It will be seen, especially in the last three chapters of this book, that the theoretical formulations which have been traditionally applied to the music of earlier composers are not always adequate in describing the music of the last hundred years, and that the conceptions embodied in the term "tonality" — even in many cases the term itself — are problematical when applied to a large portion of today's music. What should be kept in mind is that the basic relations between tones remain the same, but musical theory, which is simply the attempt accurately to describe musical effects, changes inevitably as music itself changes. Technical principles descriptive of today's music have not, in the opinion of the author, yet been adequately formulated, and it seems unlikely that they will be so formulated for many years. In a very real sense this has been true of every period in the history of music, but it is perhaps especially true of our own time, which in some respects resembles that period, before Bach, in which the concept of tonality originally arose. In any case a thorough understanding of the principles of tonality, gained through practice, observation, and experience, is an absolutely indispensable preparation for the understanding of today's musical problems.

CHAPTER

TWO

The Primary Triads
I, IV, and V

1. STRUCTURE AND CLASSIFICATION OF TRIADS

Upon examining the table of consonances on pages 15–16, we see that the major triad contains only consonant intervals, and, with inversions, contains all of the consonant intervals.

If a triad is built on each of the degrees of the major scale, using only the tones of the diatonic scale, it will be

FIG. 20

C   I   II   III   IV   V   VI   VII

found that the triads thus obtained fall into three types: major, minor, and diminished.

As we have seen already (p. 7) the triads I, IV, and V (the tonic, subdominant, and dominant) are all *major* triads, so called because the middle tone is a major third higher than the lowest tone, and the highest tone is a perfect fifth higher than the lowest tone.

We speak, in fact, of the *"third"* and the *"fifth"* of a triad, in order to identify the tones regardless of their relative positions in any given instance. The tone on which the triad is built is in like manner always known as the *"root"* of the chord. The following examples should make this clear:

FIG. 21

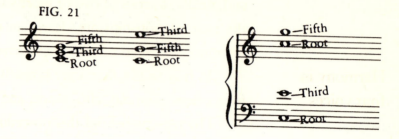

Referring again to Figure 20, we see that in all of the triads except VII the fifth is perfect, while in VII the fifth is diminished. In II, III, VI, and VII, the third is minor.

II, III, and VI are known as *"minor triads"* — that is, the perfect fifth encloses a minor third instead of, as in the major triad, a major third. The minor triad, like the major triad, contains only consonant intervals; in fact, with inversions, it too contains all of them, even though the minor third is not one of the first six partials.

VII, with its minor third and diminished fifth, is called a *"diminished triad."*

Harmonic function and root progression

It will be noted that the Roman numerals which were applied to the various degrees of the scale in Chapter One are here applied to the triads of which these degrees are the roots. This is in fact the real meaning of the Roman numerals. The numeral "I" refers not only to a tone as such, but to the *harmonic function* which we call the "tonic"; therefore it also refers to the tonic triad, since the latter is an elaboration of the tonic degree, and also of its function. In simpler language, "I" designates the *tonic harmony*, "v" the *dominant harmony*, and so forth. Chords thus designated are known as *"root chords"*; the harmonic relationships between them are called *"root relationships"*; and, finally, a series of two or more such chords, in which the root relationships are clearly an important factor in the music, is called a *"root progression."*

Harmony in four voices

As it is taught, harmony is nearly always written for four voices: soprano, alto, tenor, and bass.

The reasons behind this procedure are pedagogical, and by no means entirely arbitrary. First of all, by writing in "voices" — the word "voice" and the designations "soprano," "alto," etc. referring in this connection to the single parts, without reference to a specifically vocal or instrumental medium — the student will never lose sight of the necessity for clear and consequent voice leading, which is as indispensable an element of good harmonic writing as is the appropriate choice of chords: in fact, as will be seen later, voice leading is often a decisive factor governing the choice of chords. It must also be stressed that the elements of voice leading and of the linear [1] or melodic design from which good voice leading results, are always present, even when — as, for instance, in much writing for the piano — they do not take the form of obvious part-writing. This amounts to saying that the ear of the listener demands that one note follow another in a convincing manner, even at points in the music which do not claim the foreground of his attention. Writing in defi-

---

[1] The term "line" (adj. "linear") is used in this book to denote the progression of a single voice; "melody" (adj. "melodic") is used in its most generally understood sense — i.e., that of a line, generally in the uppermost voice, which is in the foreground of the music and is decisive in giving the latter its character.

nitely conceived voices is therefore an extremely valuable introduction to the handling of chords.

Secondly, four voices are on the whole easier to manipulate than either a smaller or a larger number of voices would be. Since a complete chord contains at least three tones, it can easily be seen, even at this point, that three-voiced writing would restrict the student in a way that would make very real, and for the purposes of harmonic study quite irrelevant, difficulties. A tone could be doubled only in cases where it was satisfactory to use an incomplete chord, while at the same time the number of positions possible for a given complete chord in three voices would be restricted to two (e.g., the C major triad). Three-voiced writing also — partly in consequence of the above — would allow only a very restricted movement of the voices, which the student would find immensely difficult until he had gained considerable command of counterpoint and considerable resourcefulness in the elaboration of harmonies through linear or melodic means.

As for writing in five or more voices, this would create unnecessary difficulties through what is often described as "denseness of texture." The movement of the voices would be restricted because of lack of space between them, thus presenting the student, in this case also, with difficulties which would be irrelevant to elementary harmonic study.

It is advisable, in solving harmony exercises, to stay within the compass of each voice, as if one were writing for human voices.

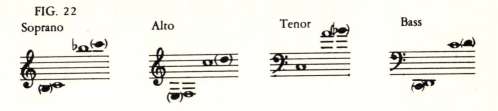

FIG. 22

The above represent, in each case, generally recognized "standard compasses," although it should be realized that actual voices differ in compass. The object of writing the voices in compass is to keep the part-writing within reasonable bounds. Certain of the exercises in this book, however, lead the soprano or the bass voice beyond the above limits. The reason for these extensions is that, since music is written for instruments as well as for voices, the student can profit by some experience in dealing with some of the problems which a somewhat freer melodic line makes necessary.

The use of four voices makes it necessary to double one of the tones of a triad, since the latter contains only three tones. For the present only the *root* may be doubled.

Note to the student

The student should clearly understand, from the very beginning, what "rules" in harmony actually imply. "Rules" are to be understood as working principles designed, at each point, to help the student to grasp the material more easily and to avoid the more obvious awkwardnesses; in no sense should they be interpreted as fundamental laws of art. It is easy to find instances, in the works of the very greatest composers, where "rules" have been broken — and easy to understand that these "violations" were neither oversights nor, for the most part, exceptional flights of genius. They are, however, cases in which the specific awkwardnesses were either "canceled out" by other aspects of the musical design, or, as it were, given character and significance as an integral part of the musical idea.

The best advice for the student is that he should feel bound by each given rule, either until further study has qualified it out of existence (see for example p. 51 in regard to doubling of the root), or, in the case of a rule of more general application, until he has mastered it thoroughly. When he has become thoroughly aware of the effect of whatever the rule prescribes or forbids, and thoroughly resourceful in the technical means involved, he should forget about the rule and remain simply free to produce or avoid the effect.

In this book an effort has been made to specifically modify or abandon rules as soon as it becomes appropriate to do so.

Close and open positions

The *positions* of the triad in four voices are classified as *"close"* or *"open."* In the close positions the three upper voices are as close together as possible, i.e., no tone of the chord can be inserted between soprano or alto, or between alto and tenor. The positions are also named after

FIG. 23

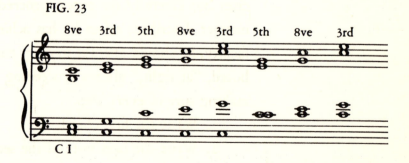

the tone which occurs in the uppermost voice, as follows: octave (or root) position, third position, and fifth position.

In the open positions one tone of the triad can be added between soprano and alto, and between alto and tenor.

FIG. 24

Exercise

Write at least five different major or minor triads in C, each in all six positions (three close and three open).

2.
CONNECTING THE PRIMARY TRIADS

The following directions should be followed by the student in his first exercises, in which he is to connect the tonic with the dominant and with the subdominant (I–V, V–I, I–IV, and IV–I). The student should work the exercises out carefully on paper, proceeding slowly in the manner described; when he has achieved a measure of facility, he should attempt to carry them out at the keyboard, "at sight," always proceeding very carefully and making sure of every step.

1. Write the first chord.

2. Write the bass note of the second chord, which

may be either higher or lower than the bass of the first chord.

(N.B. If the tenor and bass of the first chord are in unison or a third apart, however, as in the following positions, the bass tone of the second chord must be *lower*

FIG. 25

C I-V   I-IV

than that of the first chord. Otherwise it will either be impossible to connect the chords properly, or, in the case of the following, an awkward overlapping of the tenor and bass voices will result. Such connections will oc-

FIG. 26

C I-IV

casionally occur in longer series of harmonies, but should be avoided by the student at this point.)

3. Hold over into the second chord the tone which the two chords have in common.

4. Move each of the two remaining voices one degree ("stepwise") to the two remaining tones of the second chord.

FIG. 27

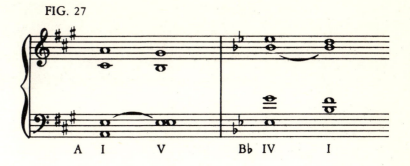

Exercises

1. Write I–V in each of the six positions, in at least two different major keys.

2. Write I–IV in all six positions, using two other keys.

3. Write V–I and IV–I in all six positions, using two new keys for each.

Types of motion

At this point the student should begin to be aware of the effects produced by the various types of motion between the voices, which are classified as follows:

1. *"Direct motion"* — also known as "similar motion" — is the movement of voices in the same direction, either up or down.

FIG. 28

If voices in direct motion move the same number of diatonic degrees, the term *"parallel motion"* is used.

FIG. 29

2. *"Oblique motion"* indicates that one voice moves while another remains stationary.

FIG. 30

3. *"Contrary motion"* indicates the movement of voices in opposite directions.

FIG. 31

It is hardly necessary to point out that, while any number of voices, theoretically at least, can move in parallel or direct motion, the same is not true of the other two types of motion. In three or more voices, the alternatives will therefore be: direct motion of all the voices; and a mixture of the various types of motion.

It is sometimes said that contrary motion is preferable to the other types of motion. Such a statement is misleading if it is taken to imply that the other types of motion should be avoided altogether. It is, of course, not so simple as that: the real point is that contrary motion is more varied and hence richer in effect than the other types of motion, but that consistent and unrelieved contrary motion will nevertheless become monotonous and overstrained if it is continued for too long. As usual, there is no substitute for observation and awareness on the part of the student.

Connecting
IV and V

Since IV and V lie on successive degrees of the scale, they have no tones in common. The procedure in connecting them is therefore somewhat different from that outlined on pages 37–38, namely:

1. Write the first chord. *N.B.:* If IV is to be connected with V, the tenor must not double the bass in unison: the open third and the close fifth positions cannot be used, therefore, unless the tenor and bass voices are an octave apart.

FIG. 32

2. The bass note of the second chord should move one step up or down, not skip a seventh, i.e.:

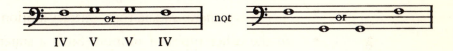

IV   V   V   IV   not

3. Move the three upper voices in contrary motion to the bass, each to the nearest tone of the second chord.

FIG. 33

Ab   IV   V   D   V   IV

Exercises

1. Connect IV–V and V–IV, each in two different major keys, using all six positions in each case.

2. Write each of the following three times, beginning each time with a different position:

1. B I–V–I	5. A I–IV–V–I–IV–I
2. Eb I–IV–I	6. Db I–V–IV–I–V–I
3. D I–IV–I–V–I	7. F# I–V–I–IV–V–I
4. Gb IV–V–I	8. Ab I–V–IV–I–IV–V–I

Connecting primary triads in the minor mode

In the minor mode — of which consideration in detail will be deferred until Chapter Four — the tonic (I) and the subdominant (IV) are minor triads. The dominant (V) contains the seventh degree, and, as we have already seen (p. 24), this degree must be chromatically raised by a semitone if it is to function as a "leading tone." For the present this procedure must be regarded as invariable: the dominant (V) thus becomes a major triad. Comparing the following will make clear the reasons for this.

FIG. 34

The student must therefore make certain that the third of the dominant chord, in the minor mode, is always preceded by the correct accidental: #, ♮, or ✕, depending on the key in question. In this connection he will find it helpful to read over the remarks (pp. 25–26) in regard to the chromatic scale.

Exercises

Work in three different positions:

1. b I–IV–I–V–I   5. a I–V–IV–V–I–IV–V–I
2. d I–IV–V–I   6. c V–I–V–IV–I–IV–V–I
3. c# IV–I–V–IV–I–V–I   7. g# IV–V–IV–I–I*–IV–V–I
4. bb V–IV–I–V–I–IV–V–I   8. eb V–I–IV–V–IV–I–V–I

* Change of position.

3.
CONNECTING PRIMARY TRIADS WITH FREER VOICE LEADING

It is possible now to depart somewhat from the restricted voice leading allowed up to this point. The methods used so far constitute the simplest and most logical manner of connecting chords taken as such, which means ignoring consideration of the melodic design and aiming simply at the smoothest possible movement from one chord to another. These methods actually represent a kind of norm which can and should be applied literally in a great number of cases; even when they are not applied literally, the principles involved still may form a basis of procedure. To achieve smooth harmonic writing, it is always a safe principle to hold over connecting tones and to move others by as small an interval as possible, as long as no melodic design is involved. From comparison of the following two examples it can easily be seen what advantages may sometimes be gained through a little more flexibility:

FIG. 35 *(a)*   *(b)*

Bb   I   V   I   IV   I   V   I

In example (b) the first and last two chords are connected more freely than before; as a result, the soprano part (i.e., the melodic line) gains some semblance of musical shape.

For the present, such treatment should be adopted as discreetly as possible, and the following general principles should be applied very carefully in order to gain acceptable results.

General considerations

1. The outer voices (for present purposes, always the soprano and bass) give music its essential character and shape, and should at all times be satisfactory in construction; that is, they should move smoothly, avoid undue repetition, and form an effective relationship with each other.

2. In the soprano part, stepwise movement should be the general rule. Skips larger than a third should be used sparingly, and should be compensated by an immediate turning of the line in the opposite direction from the skip.

In the bass part, skips will occur more frequently, since the bass contains the foundation of the harmony. But successive skips in the same direction which form a broken seventh or ninth, e.g.: are to be avoided.

3. If necessary, the highest tone and the lowest tone in the soprano voice may be held from one chord to another, but it is better not to repeat either the highest or the lowest tone after that tone has been left. Monotony resulting from repetition of the same tone on accented or unaccented beats should be avoided as far as possible.

4. In both soprano and bass, repetition of identical patterns formed by the same two or three tones should be avoided, e.g.:

5. The inner voices should move as little as possible, and common tones should be held, provided that this does not result in too large a skip in one of the other voices. Stepwise progression, in inner voices, is also preferred to large skips, which tend to attract the attention away from the more important outer parts and to detract from the smoothness of effect.

Skips of an augmented fourth or a diminished fifth

6. The skip of an augmented fourth from the fourth to the seventh degree, or vice versa, should generally be avoided in any voice. These two degrees, however, may follow each other provided the interval used is that of the diminished fifth, and provided the melodic line immediately changes direction, e.g.:

FIG. 36

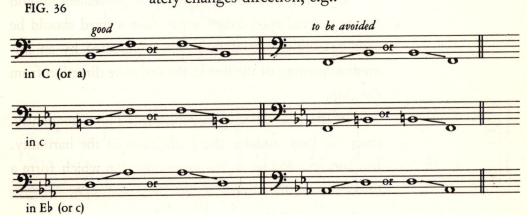

Voice leading of the leading tone

7. In the soprano voice, the leading tone should never be the highest tone of the melody; if it is followed by a lower tone, the line must eventually move to some tone higher than the leading tone. In the minor mode, the raised seventh degree must always be directly followed by the tonic; the sixth degree must not (for the present) move to the seventh degree.

Relative movement of voices

8. Good writing generally entails a prevalent tendency toward contrary motion (p. 40), with a variety of oblique and direct motion in cases where contrary motion is not possible. It is therefore best to avoid, if possible, the direct motion of all four voices at the same time, especially when large skips (movement of any voice more than a third) are involved for the upper voices, or when each of the voices moves more than one degree.

While such considerations belong more properly in the sphere of counterpoint, the effort must at all times be made to keep voice leading in mind as a very important factor in the total effect of harmonic writing.

Consecutive fifths, octaves, and unisons

9. Parallel movement of any two voices in fifths, octaves, or unisons is incorrect, except as qualified later.

For the present, all consecutive fifths or octaves, even by contrary motion, are to be avoided, as are consecutive unisons. Examples of parallel fifths, octaves, and unisons, with corrections:

FIG. 37

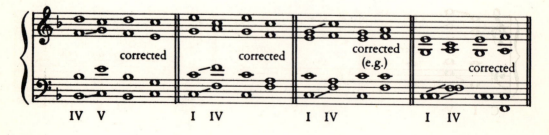

corrected   corrected   corrected
                                       (e.g.)
                                                   corrected

IV   V   I   IV   I   IV   I   IV

Note that the term "consecutive," used in regard to fifths, octaves, and unisons, refers to voices which *move*, not to tones which are held or repeated. For example,

C   I   IV

is correct, since the octave C–C (tenor and soprano voices) remains stationary.

Examples of consecutive fifths and octaves by contrary motion, with corrections:

FIG. 38

c   I   IV   IV   I

10. Fifths and octaves formed by the two outer voices must not be introduced by direct motion unless the upper voice moves stepwise while the bass skips. In such cases it is advisable if possible to hold one of the inner voices through the progression, in order to achieve a degree of contrast.

FIG. 39

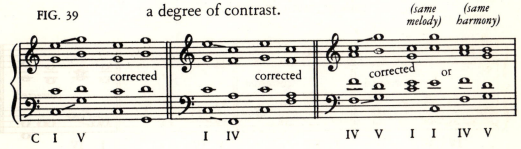

C   I   V   I   IV   IV   V   I   I   IV   V

Exercises

Bass parts to be harmonized. Repeated or held notes may be harmonized by two different positions of the same chord.

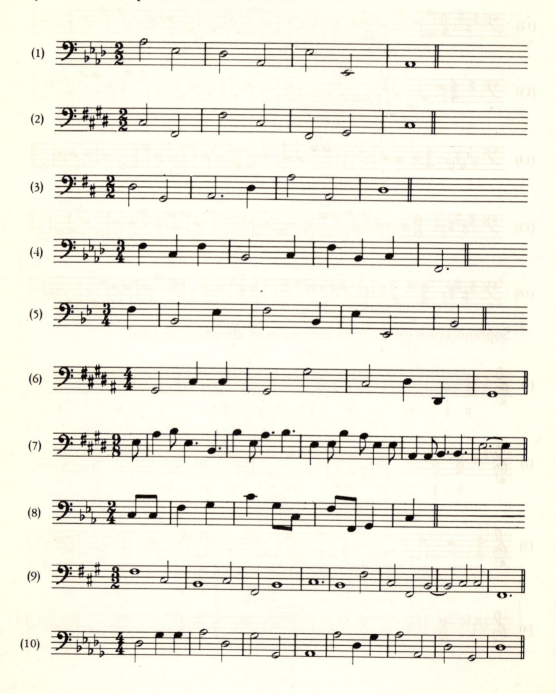

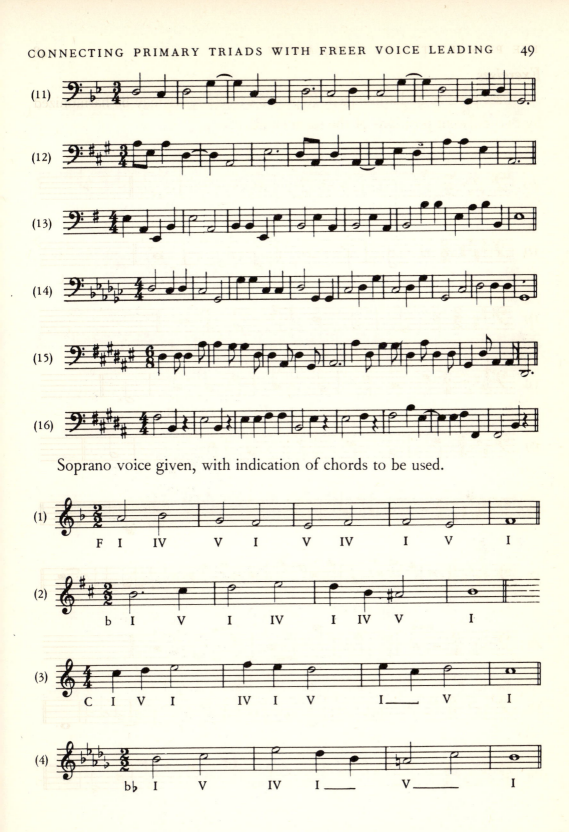

Soprano voice given, with indication of chords to be used.

(5) A I V I IV V I IV I V V I V IV I V I

(6) g I__ V IV I IV V__ IV I IV I V I

(7) F♯ I I· IV V I IV I V__ I__ IV I

V I IV I____ V I V I IV I__ IV V I

(8) c ⁊· I IV I V I V__ IV I V__ I__ V__

I IV I V I IV I IV V I IV I

Soprano voice given, no chords indicated.

(1) D♭

(2) f♯

(3) A♭

* Consecutive fifths by contrary motion are permissible here.

4. DOUBLED-THIRD, DOUBLED-FIFTH, AND TRIPLED-ROOT POSITIONS

In the following exercises, departures are made from the usual doubling of the root. It will be seen that this procedure —

1. Is sometimes unavoidable in the interests of correct or smooth voice leading.

2. Makes it possible in certain cases for the tones of the chord to be held in the inner voices, while the soprano part breaks the chord — thus avoiding the heaviness of effect produced by mechanically and literally carried out changes of position, e.g.:

FIG. 40

instead of

Third doubled   Root tripled
(Fifth omitted)

Three variations are possible:

1. Doubled fifth.

FIG. 41

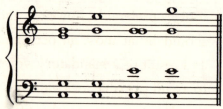

2. Doubled third.

FIG. 42

3. Tripled root, with fifth omitted.

FIG. 43

The doubled third is generally regarded as the least satisfactory arrangement of the triad, though more satisfactory in the minor than in the major triad. *The third of V — the leading tone — should never be doubled.*

Neither the third nor the fifth should be doubled in the final chord of a phrase.

The fifth may be omitted and the root tripled, as in Figure 43, at any time, in the interests of good voice leading or of less rigid movement. Such a position is acceptable as a concluding chord; the strengthened root makes the position more suitable for this purpose than the doubled third or fifth. The complete chord (with doubled root) is preferable, however, and the tripled-root position should be at most an occasional isolated form adopted as a result of a mandatory voice progression, or in order to avoid palpable awkwardness in voice leading.

No tone except the fifth of the chord should be omitted; the third must always be present.

Spacing of voices

The student should follow carefully the general rule that soprano and alto, and alto and tenor, should not in any chord lie more than an octave apart. Occasionally, owing to a large skip in the soprano, it may be in the interests of good voice leading to relax this rule temporarily, e.g.:

I   I   IV   V

In such a case the voices must be immediately led closer together — if possible, in the chord directly following.

Very exceptionally, and again in the interests of good voice leading, it may prove advisable to cross the soprano and alto voices, or the alto or tenor voices, e.g.:

In this case, too, the voices should be led immediately back to their normal positions.

The student should never, for the present, make use of this device if he can find another solution which is acceptable; and in no case should he lead one of the upper voices below the bass.

The exercises should be done with special care, careful examination of the reasons for the procedures indicated, and careful choice of the position in the opening chord which makes possible the most satisfactory solution.

Exercises

Double or triple tones as indicated.

* Doubled third.

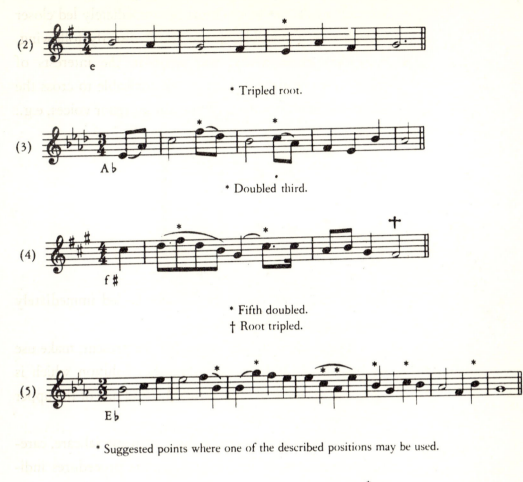

(2)

e

* Tripled root.

(3)

Ab

* Doubled third.

(4)

f#

* Fifth doubled.
† Root tripled.

(5)

Eb

* Suggested points where one of the described positions may be used.

(6)

c#   (IV)   (IV)

* See Exercise 5.

(7)

F

* See Exercise 5.

In the following three exercises, no indications are given. The exercises should be worked out with the utmost care for a good choice of chords, and for good voice leading.

N.B. The leading tone (third of v) is *never* to be doubled, either in the major or as an altered tone in the minor.

The limitations of chord figuration

In the figuration of chords, the Roman numerals I–VII have been explained as referring to the position and function of the roots within the key; in the next chapter, Arabic numerals will be introduced, which refer to the inner structure of chords. The musical practice — including analysis as well as composition — of the nineteenth and especially of the twentieth century has made it clear that the final adequacy of such figuration is more than problematical, and that figuration must be regarded as a practical convenience rather than as a completely accurate indication of what is heard in the music. In the sections of this book dealing with "frozen accessory tones" (Chapter Seven), and with "chromatic harmony" (Chapters Twelve and Thirteen), some of the problems involved will be dealt with more fully than would be relevant at this point in the work.

The terms in question, however, have been in such universal use for such a long period that there is little sense, short of a radically new formulation of harmonic fact and harmonic theory, in attempting to modify them. Such attempts at modification as the author has seen seem to suffer from the same type of inadequacy, when viewed in the light of what the ear actually hears, as the traditional nomenclature, and to be doubly misleading because, not only failing to overcome the insufficiencies of the latter, they tend to compound them. He therefore has adopted the traditional symbols without hesitation, recognizing their limitations but accepting them as conventional terms, subject to qualification and reinterpretation through sharpened awareness of what is actually heard in music.

CHAPTER

THREE

I_6, IV_6, and V_6

1. THE SIX–CHORD

Six-chords are so-called "first inversions" of triads in which the third, not the root, is in the bass, e.g.:

C I_6

While the notes are designated as before — root, third, and fifth — the intervals are, of course, different; and the Arabic numeral 6 (e.g., I_6) denotes the interval of a sixth which the root, in one or more of the upper voices, forms with the third in the bass. Since the fifth is still above the third in this chord and, therefore, forms with it the interval of a third, a complete indication would be, for example, I_3^6. But, exactly because the relationship of the fifth and third is the same in the six-chord as in the triad in root position, and because it is therefore only the sixth which gives the six-chord its character, only the one figure (6) is commonly used.

The six-chord is the only chord except the triad which is considered as completely consonant and, therefore, is unrestricted in use. In a very rough sense it is less emphatic and less conclusive than the triad from which it is derived (called sometimes its "fundamental position"). The student must learn by experience to gain a feeling for such differences. For the present he must simply consider the six-chord unsuitable as the concluding chord of a phrase or exercise.

Uses of the six-chord

The uses of the six-chord may be roughly summarized as follows:

1. By providing less emphatic forms of the harmonies in question, it not only adds new resources to the harmonic vocabulary but allows for subtler contrasts of emphasis.

2. Since the third degree of the scale forms the bass of I_6, the sixth degree that of IV_6, and the seventh degree that of V_6, the six-chord adds three new bass tones to those already available (the first, fourth, and fifth degrees). This makes forms of progression possible in which, by the use of the six-chord, a skip in the bass is reduced or eliminated, and in which the more emphatic triad is juxtaposed to the less emphatic six-chord, thus obtaining a degree of contrast in emphasis, e.g.:

FIG. 44

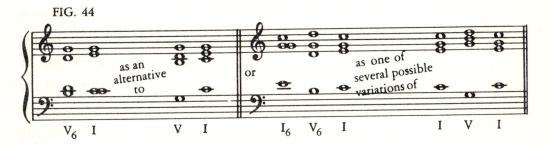

For the present, either the root or the fifth of the six-chord may be doubled.

FIG. 45

Positions of C I₆

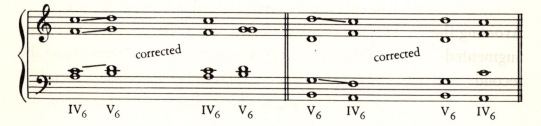

Parallel octaves, fifths, and unisons must be avoided as always; for this, special care will often be required, e.g.:

FIG. 46

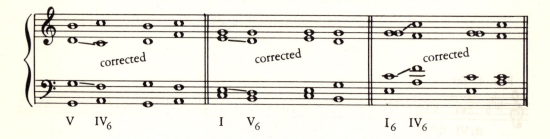

IV₆ V₆   IV₆ V₆   V₆ IV₆   V₆ IV₆

corrected   corrected

V   IV₆   I   V₆   I₆ IV₆

corrected   corrected   corrected

Exercises

At least four different positions should be used for each exercise, including both doubled-root and doubled-fifth positions of the six-chord.

1. C I–I₆   4. B♭ I₆–I
2. F I–IV₆   5. B I₆–IV
3. G I–V₆   6. E♭ I₆–V

7. A IV–I$_6$

8. A♭ IV–V$_6$

(N.B. Caution in bass part!)

9. E V–I$_6$

10. D♭ V–IV$_6$

11. B IV$_6$–I

12. G♭ IV$_6$–V

13. F♯ V$_6$–I

14. C♭ V$_6$–IV

(N.B. Caution in bass part!)

15. B I$_6$–IV$_6$

16. D♭ I$_6$–V$_6$

17. E IV$_6$–I$_6$

18. A♭ IV$_6$–V$_6$

19. A V$_6$–I$_6$

20. E♭ V$_6$–IV$_6$

2. ALTERED DEGREES IN THE MINOR MODE

In the minor mode, the resources available may now be enlarged by careful attention to the following:

Avoiding the augmented second

If the sixth degree of the scale moves in any voice directly to the raised seventh, this sixth degree must also be raised a semitone, in order to avoid the awkward interval of an augmented second which otherwise results (see (a) below).

For the same reason, the seventh degree, if it moves downward to the sixth degree, must for the present remain unaltered whether or not the latter is altered (see (b) and (c) below).

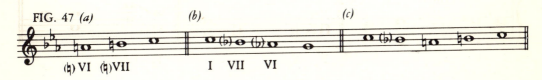

FIG. 47 *(a)*   *(b)*   *(c)*

(♮) VI (♮)VII   I   VII   VI

Neither the altered sixth degree (the third of IV) nor the altered seventh degree (the third of V) may be doubled. When these degrees are unaltered either tone may be doubled as the context demands.

Alterations and the "melodic minor scale"

It will be seen from this that the minor scale, in practice, has two forms between the fifth degree and the upper octave: the ascending form, which contains the raised sixth and seventh degrees; and the descending form, in which these degrees remain unaltered. While the ascending form of the scale is indispensable for reasons of articulation and emphasis, which will be fully discussed later, the character of the minor mode as such demands that the unaltered tones — i.e., the descending form of the scale — be also frequently introduced. The reason for this is that the ascending form is identical with the corresponding portion of the major scale.

The above principles embody everything that is conveyed by the commonly used term "melodic minor scale," illustrated below:

FIG. 48

Since the actual usage in music is rather free, and since the above rules are subject to later modification, it is preferred here to consider the alterations of the sixth and seventh degrees as individual, though commonly applied, instances, instead of regarding them as ingredients of a fixed scale formula.

These principles apply only to the voices directly involved; no tone is affected by altered or unaltered tones occurring in other voices, e.g.:

FIG. 49

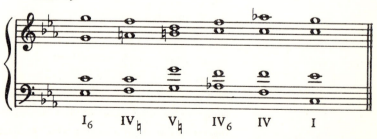

Figuration of altered tones

Altered tones are indicated in the "figuration" of chords as follows: When the root is altered, the "accidental" (p. 25) which specifies the alteration is placed before the Roman numeral which indicates the chord in question, e.g.:

c ♮VI ♮VII

When the third is altered in a triad,[1] the accidental is placed below the Roman numeral, to the right, e.g.:

c IV♮   a V♯

When any tone other than the third is altered, the accidental is placed in the same position, followed by the Arabic numeral which indicates that tone, e.g.:

c II♮5   g♯ III×5

In six-chords and all chords other than triads in the fundamental position,[1] an accidental which is not followed by an Arabic figure refers to the bass tone, e.g.:

c II 6/4 ♮

---

[1] Or any chord derived from the triad, in fundamental position (see Chapter Six and pp. 224 ff.). *N.B.* This is a slight variant of the procedure used in traditional bass figuration, where an accidental not followed by a figure always refers to the third of the chord. The author feels justified in suggesting this to cover cases in which no actual bass is given, and in which an alteration in the bass tone must therefore be indicated in the figuration.

If in such chords the third is altered, the figure 3 must follow the accidental, e.g.:

a   III$^6_{\sharp 3}$

Though all these principles will apply eventually to all voices, no attempt should be made in the exercises immediately following to adopt progressions in which alterations occur in voices other than the bass — specifically in the progressions IV₆–V₆–I, and I–V₆–IV₆, e.g.:

FIG. 50

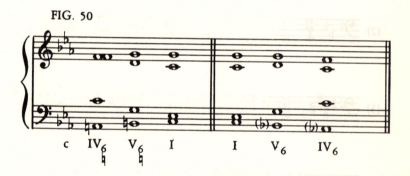

c   IV₆   V₆   I   I   V₆   IV₆

Exercises

Minor mode only.

1. c♯ I–V₆–IV₆–V♯–I
2. f V–IV$^6_♮$–V$^6_♮$–I–IV–I
3. b♭ I–V₆–IV$^6_♮$–V$^6_♮$–I
4. a I–IV₆–V–IV$^6_♯$–V$^6_♯$–I

Both major and minor modes.

5. E♭ I–V₆–IV₆–I–IV–V–I
6. f♯ I–IV₆–V♯–IV–I₆–V$^6_♯$–I
7. D♭ I₆–IV–V–IV₆–I–V₆–V–I

8. g♯♯ I–V$_{♯}^{6}$–IV$_6$–V$_※$–IV$_{♯}^{6}$–V$_※^{6}$–I

9. A I–V$_6$–I–IV$_6$–I$_6$–IV–V–I

10. b♭ I–V$_♮$–IV$_6$–I$_6$–V$_♮$–IV–I–V$_♮^{6}$–I

11. E I–V$_6$–IV$_6$–V–IV–IV$_6$–I

12. c I–IV$_♮^{6}$–V$_♮^{6}$–I–IV$_6$–V$_♮$–I

13. B I–V$_6$–I–IV–V–V$_6$–I

14. f IV$_6$–V$_♮$–I–IV–I$_6$–V$_♮$–IV$_♮^{6}$–V$_♮^{6}$–I

Figured basses.

Soprano voice, with chords indicated.

* Third doubled.

Soprano voice, no chords indicated.

(1)

(2)

(3)

(4)

(5)

(6)

(IV₆)

(7)

(8)

(9)

(10)

CHAPTER

FOUR

The Consonant Diatonic
Harmonies of the
Major and Minor Modes

1. SECONDARY
TRIADS AND
SIX–CHORDS
IN THE
MAJOR MODE

The triads on the second, third, sixth, and seventh degrees (II, III, VI, and VII) are, in order to distinguish them from the primary triads I, IV, and V, known as *secondary triads*. In the major mode, II, III, and VI are minor triads; VII is a diminished triad and for this reason needs special attention (p. 75).

Positions and doublings of II, III, and VI are the same as those of the primary triads I, IV, and V. Other doublings are also possible; however, the fifth of III, being the leading tone, should not be doubled in the "fundamental" (root-bass) position, at present.

FIG. 51

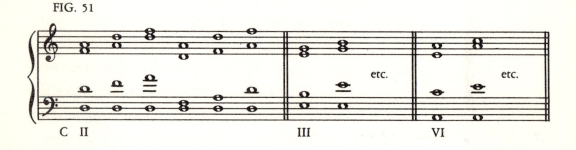

C II   III   VI

2. BASIC RELATIONSHIPS BETWEEN HARMONIES

The use of the complete set of triads raises at this point the question of harmonic relationships within the diatonic limits of the key. Although this is something which can be ultimately learned only through much experience, observation, and practice, the following observations can be made now and should prove a help as a preliminary point of departure:

1. Relationships between harmonies may be classified in three general types, according to the interval between roots in the fundamental position: the relationship of the *fifth* (as between I and V, I and IV, II and VI, etc.); of the *second* (as between IV and V); and of the *third* (as between I and III, II and IV, etc.).

2. As in the case of the primary triads, chords in the relationship of the fifth — always assuming that no altered tones are present — have one tone in common; those in the relationship of the second have no tones in common. Chords in the relationship of the fifth are normally connected in the same way as I and V, or I and IV; chords in the relationship of a second are normally connected in the same way as IV and V. (See pp. 39 ff.)

3. Chords in the relationship of the third have two tones in common, and are connected as follows: the root is doubled in both chords; the bass is moved a third (not, for the present, a sixth in the opposite direction); the two common tones are held over; and the remaining voice is moved to the remaining tone of the second chord, which will always be one step in contrary motion to the movement of the bass, e.g.:

FIG. 52

I   III   I   III   I   VI   I   VI

In the following exercises, the strict rules given for the connection of triads should be observed in all cases.

Exercises

Secondary and primary triads in root progression.

1. A I–III–VI–IV–II–V–I
2. B♭ I–VI–V–IV–I–II–V–I
3. G I–II–VI–IV–V–III–II–V–I
4. D♭ I–IV–II–III–VI–IV–V–I
5. E I–V–III–II–VI–III–IV–I
6. A♭ VI–II–V–I–III–VI–IV–I
7. D I–III–II–VI–III–IV–V–I
8. F V–III–I–IV–II–VI–III–V–IV–I

3. ROOT RELATIONSHIPS

Relationship of the fifth

Characteristics of the different root progressions or relationships (p. 32) may now be observed in accordance with the character of the interval between the roots, and the degree of contrast between the two chords themselves.

First in order comes the relationship of the fifth, because of the primacy of this interval in the triad, and hence in the whole complex of relationship on which our musical hearing is based. Whether in any given case the actual movement is that of a fifth or of its inversion, the fourth, depends on the context and is immaterial as far as the character of the relationship is concerned, except as noted in the next paragraph. In the classic harmonic style, harmonic movement by fifths plays an overwhelmingly large role — so much so in fact that it will sometimes be found useful to conceive the series of descending fifths in the diatonic scale (I–IV–VII–III–VI–II–V–I) as a kind of harmonic scale from which deviations are considered as variants or contractions in the normal harmonic flow. For present purposes such theoretical conceptions may be deferred in favor of the observation that the progression of the fifth, characterized by a single common tone and a large interval, contains the two elements of relationship and contrast to a greater degree than is the case with the progression of the third or of the second.

Careful note should be taken of the contrast in effect between the rising and the falling progressions of the fifth. In the rising progression the root of the second chord is already present as the fifth of the first chord; in the falling progression it is the root of the first chord which is held over to become the fifth of the second chord. It is obvious, therefore, that the falling progression brings a greater degree of contrast than the rising progression, since in the falling progression the root of the second chord is a fresh element. Secondly — possibly because of the relationships created by the overtone series — the lower fifth seems to take on something of the aspect of a fundamental tone, and the upper fifth that of an overtone, with the result that it is sometimes necessary to plan harmonic progressions in such a way that the lower fifth does not produce an undesired effect of a new tonic harmony. An attentive comparison of the two progressions should make this clear.

FIG. 53

I   V   I   IV   I   V   I   IV

Compare also the following:

FIG. 54 *(a)*   *(b)*

(C – G)   (C – F)

C   I   VI   V₆   VI₆   C   I   VI   II
         G   I₆   II   V   I   F   III VI   IV   VII₆   I

The two examples in Figure 54 illustrate in the most vivid form — that of actual change of key (*modulation* — see Chapter Nine) — the respective relationships of the upper and the lower fifth: (a) is a modulation to the key of the dominant, the upper fifth; (b) a modulation to the lower fifth — the subdominant. Both modulations are carried out with the same number of chords. But though the melodic line in (b) rises, while that in (a) falls, the modulation (b) to the subdominant will be felt as the more conclusive of the two. In other words, after the sixth chord in (a) the attentive listener will not feel quite satisfied that he has definitely changed the key: this final chord still retains some of the "dominant" feeling, and if the triad of C (in parentheses) is then played, it will seem a more satisfactory tonic than the triad of G which precedes it. The sixth chord in (b), however, gives a real sense of conclusion, and the C major triad which follows it in parentheses will tend to sound like a dominant.

It is for the above reasons that the progression of the lower fifth is regarded as a kind of norm, especially in the case of dissonant chords (p. 14), of which the diminished triad VII in the major mode is an example. The use of this triad in its fundamental position is somewhat restricted, owing to the fact that the addition of the minor or diminished seventh VII₇ in the major or minor modes respectively (pp. 160, 162, 163), intensifies the dissonant character of the chord and at the same time gives it a richer tone quality.

For the present, VII is to be used in one sense only, as follows:

FIG. 55

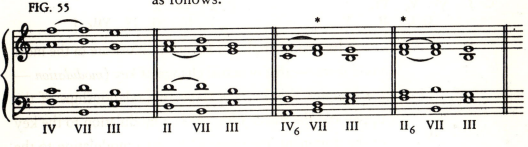

IV	VII	III	II	VII	III	IV₆	VII	III	II₆	VII	III

* Why the doubled third?

The dissonant fifth of the chord is to be "prepared," or in other words held over from the preceding chord, which must therefore be either II or IV; the fifth must also be "resolved," or in other words moved down in the same voice one step to the root of the following chord, which must therefore be III, a fifth below the root of VII.

Since VII can only take part in the secondary progression VII–III, there is no objection to doubling the seventh degree, which does not function here as a leading tone (i.e., does not proceed to the tonic).

**Relationship
of the third**

The progression of the third is in some respects analogous to the progression of the fifth, but, since the

FIG. 56

interval is smaller and since the chords have two tones instead of only one in common, the contrast is much less and the effect therefore much weaker. This is particularly noticeable in the case of the upward progression, and special attention must be paid to this progression in connection with *accent* (pp. 77 ff.).

**Relationship
of the second**

The progression of the second involves two chords which have no common tones, and in which the two roots cannot be placed in a single triad. It therefore pre-

FIG. 57

sents — as far as the actual tones of the chords are concerned — the greatest contrast possible between triads in the diatonic scale, even though the bass moves only one degree. Generally speaking, the effect of the progression should be observed in connection with the chord which immediately follows, or more rarely, the chord which immediately precedes it — so that one hears the whole progression from one metrically strong point to another. Thus, in the progression I–II–III it is the total progression of the third which is decisive, whereas in the progression I–II–VI the chord II gives to the following VI a contrast and relief which the progression I–VI, alone, would not provide.

4. HARMONY AND RHYTHM

The above facts are of the utmost importance because of their bearing on the question of rhythm. Possibly no single factor has so much importance in the achievement of good harmonic writing as rhythm.

Musicians of all times have recognized the primacy of rhythm in music, yet no aspect of music has been, and still remains, so inadequately defined. The reason for this is fairly clear. Rhythm in music includes so much that the attempt to define it in any complete sense might well result in an attempt to define music itself.

The student of harmony must at all times be strongly aware of the rhythmic effect of the harmonies which he chooses; he must in fact choose them above all with respect to their place in the "harmonic rhythm" — i.e., the rhythmic pattern formed by the chords and chord changes.

At various points in the present book, reference will be made to the question of harmonic rhythm, as new elements involving it are introduced. For the moment, the important considerations will be: first, movement as such; secondly, accent.

Movement

The student must observe, first of all, the effects which are produced by movements of different kinds. He will discover the following facts:

1. The more frequent the changes which take place within a given space of time, the more effort is required of the ear, and, therefore, the more energetic the musical effect. The converse is, of course, also true; the ear listens with less effort, and therefore with less feeling of energy

expended, to music in which changes occur less frequently.

Musicians speak, in this connection, of music which is more, or less, dense or heavy in texture; more, or less, rich in detail. Such terms may be applied either in a general and inclusive sense, or in reference to any single musical factor of movement, such as harmony, counterpoint, melody, rhythm (in the sense of individual note values), or instrumentation.

The above fact has of course an important influence not only on the character of the music but on the tempo at which it can be performed. The richer the detail (or the heavier the texture), the less suitable will be a very fast tempo, since impressions will in that case succeed each other too quickly; while the lighter the texture, the more spare the detail, the less suitable will be a very slow tempo, since the interest will in that case be insufficiently sustained.

The student should learn to apply these principles to *harmonic* movement — i.e., the varying effects of rapid or slow changes of harmony, as distinguished from the often contrasting movement of the melody. The following examples illustrate the principle involved:

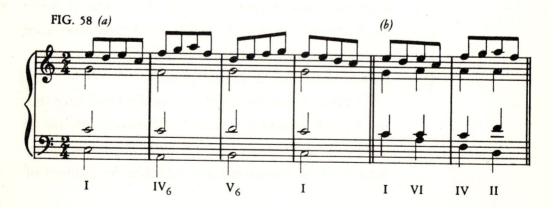

FIG. 58 (a)   (b)

I   IV$_6$ V$_6$ I   I   VI   IV   II

The melody is the same in all three examples, but clearly (b) in Figure 58 would have to be played more slowly than (a), because the harmonies change more often in (b); while (c), with a harmonic change on every eighth note, would be played even more slowly than (b).

By "changes of harmony" is, of course, meant changes which involve real harmonic contrast — that is, changes of *root*. A mere change of position, or a progression which includes only different inversions of the same root chord, involves movement of a different type.

In individual instances, it is true, a change of position may sometimes become rhythmically equivalent to a real harmonic change; generally when this is true it is the result of a striking skip in the bass, or of some other kind of vigorous contrapuntal movement. (See, for example, the first correction in Figure 59 (c).)

Certain questions which will be discussed later (pp. 200 ff.) will expand the picture of harmonic rhythm as outlined here. For the present, however, harmonic movement is to be considered as established by changes of root, and harmonic rhythm as the rhythmic pattern formed by such changes.

2. The ear demands continuity of harmonic movement, in much the same sense that it demands continuity of movement in other respects. In other words, once a pattern of harmonic movement or harmonic change has been established, the ear will be disappointed if the pattern is weakened — if the changes take place, for no apparent musical reason, less frequently than the ear has been led by the context to expect. The pattern may be intensified to a certain extent, but, except for purposes of accent or emphasis, it must not be reduced.

Since *nothing in music should become mechanical* it is, once again, impossible to lay down hard and fast rules; but the following examples of faulty harmonic rhythm — with their corrections — may help to make this point clear. In some cases, repetition of the root is corrected; in others, a tendency of the bass to bog down, after lively movement in the first measures, is corrected.

FIG. 59 (a)

I   V₆ VI III   IV I₆ IV IV   V   I   V₆ V   I

corrected

I   V₆ VI III   IV I IV II   V I V V   I

(b)

I   V   I   IV I   V   I   I   IV   I   I₆ V

corrected

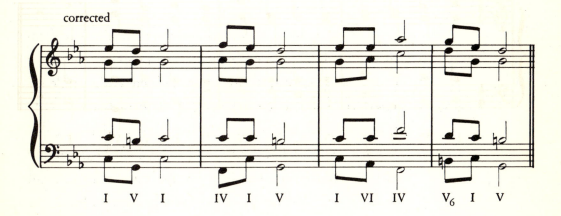

I   V   I   IV I   V   I   VI IV   V₆ I   V

$$I \quad IV_6 \, I_6 \, IV \quad IV_6 \quad I \quad V_6 \, VI \, III \quad I_6 \quad II_6 \qquad III \, VII_6 \, I \quad II_6 \quad V \quad I$$

corrected

$$I \quad IV_6 \, I_6 \, IV \quad IV_6 \quad I \quad V_6 \, VI \, III \quad I_6 \quad IV \, II \, V \quad III \, IV_6 \, I \quad II_6 \, II \, V \quad I$$

* Poor harmonic rhythm.

The principle of harmonic movement must be kept in mind at all times; the technical problems which it creates will become always more refined as the student's resources become greater. But, if the principle is clearly understood at this point — if the student, that is, cultivates a *sense* of harmonic movement instead of simply relying on rule of thumb — its application to different situations should be always essentially clear to him.

Accent   As far as the problem of accent is concerned, the student should make himself as fully aware as possible of the bearing of harmonic relationships (pp. 72–77) upon accent, and of three general types of accentuation which he must take into account if his harmonizations are to be successful: accent of weight, metrical accent, and "expressive" accent.

The term "accent," as used here, does not mean the stress which the performer should give to a specific tone or chord; this will depend on the individual instance and, if the performance is adequate, will result from the musical sense of the passage in question. Here, those "accents" are meant which are inherent in the shape the music takes, and which are present whether or not they demand special stress in performance. These inherent accents must, if the musical impression is to be clear, be underlined by *all* of the elements in the music, working, as it were, in co-ordination with each other. (Or, better still, music should be conceived, not as a sum or compound of such elements as harmony, melody, rhythm, and counterpoint, but as an organic whole of which these elements are simply different aspects.)

Regarding the relation of harmony to accent, the important fact to remember is that *accent means contrast, and vice versa*. This will be considered more specifically in connection with the various types of accent, described briefly in the paragraphs which follow.

Accent of weight   The most important type of accent, because of its vital bearing on the question of articulation, or phrasing, is what may be called the *"accent of weight."* This term denotes the principal rhythmic accent, which corresponds with the end of a musical "phrase."

A phrase may be roughly defined as that portion of a melody which progresses without interruption to a "break," either momentary or definitive. It has been found helpful, in fact, to consider it as that portion which, if it could be sung, should — ideally — be sung in one breath. This conception will serve the purpose if it is remembered (1) that there are many phrases which are too long to be sung in a single breath, and, in instrumental music, many melodies which are outside either the range or the technique of the singer, and (2) that a phrase consists not only of melody or line, but of all the factors which enter into a given musical context. It is movement and rhythm as such, and not simply melody, which constitute the principle of the phrase.

The important point is that a musical phrase, in any and all of its aspects, must be considered in terms of *tension* and *relaxation,* the moment of relaxation being that of the final accent, or what we have called the accent of weight. Everything which precedes this final accent may be considered as, so to speak, the "upbeat" of the phrase, during which the tension of the movement must be sustained; the moment of the final accent, and any tones or harmonies which follow it, may be considered as its "downbeat." *The principle of tension and relaxation is perhaps the most important single principle of musical rhythm, and its bearing on all questions of musical expression and interpretation cannot be overestimated.*

Cadences

The conclusion of a phrase may be considered from a slightly different angle, as the goal or destination toward which the phrase moves. In this sense, it is known as the *"cadence"* (note the derivation from the Italian verb *cadere,* to fall), and this term "cadence" is applied in a more restricted sense to the final harmonies of the phrase. In this connection, special note should be taken of the primary role of the tonic, dominant, and sub-dominant harmonies. This primary role is based, first, on the fact that since both IV and V are in the important relationship of the fifth to the tonic harmony, they are especially well adapted for emphasizing the tonality, and thus for "pulling the harmony together," as it is sometimes put, at its most important points. Furthermore, since the relationships between the primary harmonies are those of the second (IV–V) or of the fifth (IV–I, V–I), a requisite degree of contrast is always assured.

The cadence formulas which follow have, therefore, been classified in terms of these harmonies. While cadence formulas are infinitely varied in practice — their evolution having, in fact, played an overwhelming and fateful role in the development of music — the simpler forms given here may be taken as a point of departure.

Cadence formulas are classified in three general groups, according to the nature of the final chord of the cadence.

1. Cadences which end with I are known as *"perfect"* cadences. If the final tonic chord is preceded by V the cadence is known as *"authentic"*; V is, in this cadence, generally preceded by II or IV, e.g.:

FIG. 60

IV   V   I   II₆   V   I   II   V   I

The less commonly used formula IV–I is known as the "*plagal*" cadence; in this cadence, IV is frequently preceded by V, e.g.:

FIG. 61

| V | I₆ | IV | I | | V | VI | IV | I |

2. A cadence ending in IV or V is known as a "*half*" cadence, and is, of course, less conclusive than either of the forms of the "perfect" cadence; in this cadence, IV or V is frequently preceded by I, e.g.:

FIG. 62

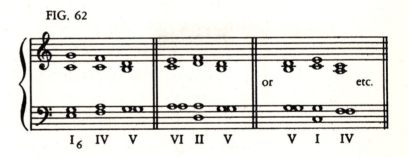

| I₆ | IV | V | | VI | II | V | | V | I | IV |

3. The "*deceptive*" cadence substitutes some other chord, generally VI or IV, for the final tonic in the authentic cadence formula; it is generally followed in a subsequent phrase group by the authentic cadence and therefore serves both as a prolongation and as an intensification of the harmonic goal. Examples of the deceptive cadence follow:

FIG. 63

IV V VI   II V VI   IV V IV₆

The final accent of a phrase may coincide either with the final chord of the cadence, in which case the phrase or the phrase ending is termed "masculine," e.g.:

FIG. 64

F I₆ IV II I₆ V   I

or it may coincide with one of the preparatory chords of the cadence, in which case we speak of a "feminine" phrase or ending, e.g.:

FIG. 65

I₆ IV II I₆ II₆   V I

The above formulas do not, of course, embody the only forms which the cadence may take. Weaker relationships, such as III–I, II–I, VII–I, or even, quite exceptionally, VI–I; half cadences on chords other than V or IV; phrase endings on inversions or even on dissonant chords (see pp. 97 ff.) — all of these are means which eventually make possible the greatest variety, and the most extreme gradation and subtlety, in the articulation of phrases. Occasional instances (e.g., Ex. 6 on p. 94; Ex. 6 and Ex. 9 on p. 96) which demand such treatment will be found in the following exercises. In general, however, the student should regard such instances as exceptional, and should aim above all, for the present, at the solidity of structure which is embodied in the generally classified forms of cadence; in other words, it will be found most helpful if he regards these as points of departure, and other forms, for the time being at least, as refinements or variations upon these.

Metrical accent   The two remaining types of accent require less extensive treatment. "*Metrical*" accent underlines the metrical structure, and generally coincides with the first beat of the measure, though, in cases where beats are regularly subdivided, the beats themselves may be considered from the same point of view as implying subsidiary metrical accents.

The eventual importance of the metrical accent depends on the individual character of the music, and it is probable that an overwhelmingly greater number of errors results from exaggerating the importance of metrical accent than from ignoring it. The significance of the "bar line" varies from that of a quite essential structural

element — as in dance music, etc. — to that of a necessary convenience for purposes of ensemble performance;
and composers of all periods since its introduction into
musical notation have used it with the greatest possible
subtlety and flexibility.

For the present the student should consider the bar
as representing a metrical division which always must be
taken into consideration, though by no means necessarily stressed; he should be careful to provide suitable
contrast, after the bar, with the harmony of the upbeat
which immediately precedes it. The beginner especially
is generally warned —

1. Not to repeat a chord across the bar line.

2. Not to hold or repeat a tone in the bass from a
"weak" over to the following "strong" beat, as long as
only consonant chords (i.e., triads and six-chords) are
involved, unless it is expressly intended to displace the
accent (see p. 90).

3. To avoid the relationship of a rising third (p. 76)
between the last chord of one measure and the first chord
of the next.

Such warnings are useful only if the student uses
them as a point of departure for awareness of the essential
musical factors involved, and not merely as a prescrip-
tion.

Expressive accentuation Finally, the student should make himself aware of
such points as require *"expressive"* accentuation. *It should
be emphasized in the strongest possible terms that expressive
accentuation is, under any circumstances, justifiable only in
terms of the contour of the music itself — which means, for
present purposes, the individual contour of the melodic line*

or of the rhythmic pattern. Melodic tones which stand out because they are longer than those which surround them may be generally considered as accented in this sense, as may tones which are the highest or the lowest in a phrase. If the latter, however, occur on the offbeat as the result of a broken chord interval, it will generally be the supporting harmony which will take the accent in question, e.g.:

FIG. 66

I   V₆ I IV₆ I₆ IV II V V₆   I

In similar fashion, rhythmically displaced or "syncopated" tones always imply expressive accentuation. Under this heading are included:

1. Tones which, occurring at a metrically weak point, are held over a following point which is metrically stronger; e.g.:

FIG. 67

I₆   I   II₆   II   V   V₆   I

2. Tones occurring on the weak part of a measure
or beat which are longer than those occurring on the
strong part of the same unit, e.g.:

FIG. 68

I   V   VI III   II₆ II V   I

3. Tones which embody a metrical pattern contrasting with that already established as the basis of the
movement, and implying longer time values.

FIG. 69

I₆ I IV   II V   I   I VII₆I₆ II I₆ II₆ V₆VII₆ I

"Expressive" accentuation as described here demands
above all the awareness of the student, and it is impossible
to lay down any reliable rules or directions regarding its
use. The principal guidepost that can be given is that
stated already on page 83 — *accent means contrast*. If the
student becomes really aware of, and develops a real sense
for, the significance of accentuation, he will find in his

steadily increasing harmonic resources the means of achieving the precise degree of emphasis needed in any specific case. In the meantime, the questions discussed on pages 72–77, and in the present section, should help to give him a preliminary insight into the nature of the problems he will meet.

Exercises

Figured basses.

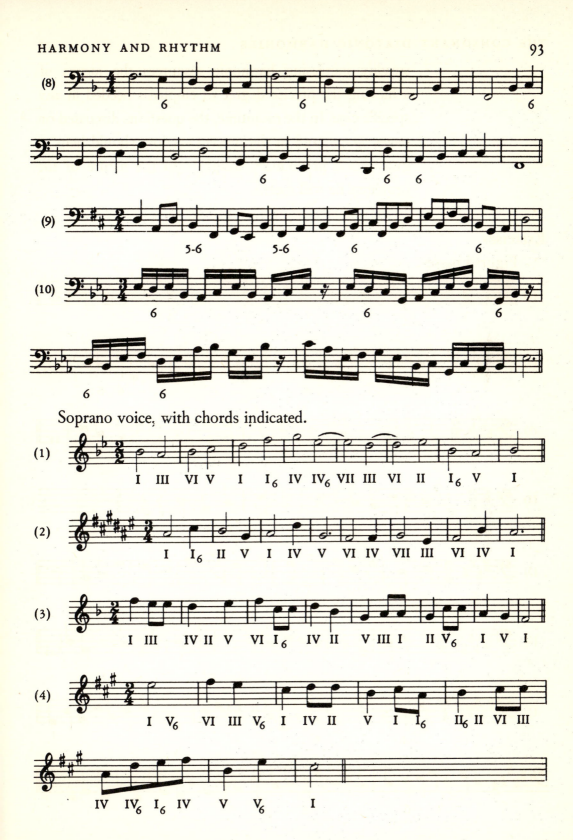

Soprano voice, with chords indicated.

Exercises using all harmonic resources covered up to this point.

(In setting the following exercises the student should first determine the phrase structure (i.e., the number of phrases, and the consequent position of the necessary cadences), and plan his cadences (pp. 84 ff.), before proceeding to the harmonization of the exercise as a whole. He should then carry out the harmonization in terms of the chosen cadences, taking care in particular to see that the line of the bass moves smoothly and logically, and that no one (or more) of the harmonies of the cadence is weakened through the use of the same harmony or chord too closely before it. In planning the cadences the student should bear in mind the fact that the ear will associate the harmonies of the cadences with each other, across the harmonies which intervene; and though this fact will create no special problems at this time, he should accustom himself to awareness of it.)

(5)

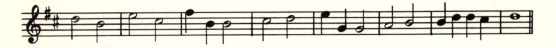

(6)

(7)

(8)

(9)

(10)

5. SIX-CHORDS OF THE SECONDARY HARMONIES

Six-chords in the secondary harmonies are used in the same manner, and with the same general type of effect, as those of the primary triads (pp. 58 ff.). In II_6 and VI_6, either root or fifth may be doubled. The same is generally true of III_6, in spite of the fact that the fifth of III is the leading tone; since even in the progression III–I the compelling force of the descending fifth in the bass is not present, the effect of the leading tone is much weaker than in the case of the progression V–I, and the leading tone, therefore, can be treated with less caution. In the case of the progression III_6–I, however, the effect of the leading tone is more problematical, and in general it is better to double the root or even, as will be seen later (p. 228), the third.

VII_6, in contrast to VII in the fundamental position (p. 75), may be treated with the same freedom as any other six-chord. This usage dates from the very earliest times, and in fact the chord will be found extremely useful as a less emphatic substitute for v in variants of the cadence formula. For the latter reason its root (the leading tone) should never be doubled; on the other hand either the third or the fifth may be doubled with good effect.

The theoretical basis for the above, as against the quite different treatment of VII in the fundamental position, lies in the fact that the diminished fifth in VII proper is a dissonance in respect to the bass, while both the minor third and the major sixth in VII_6 are consonances. While many of the grounds furnished by traditional theory in explanation of general musical usage seem suspect and even sometimes untenable, this one seems quite valid;

in any case it is the usage which is important and which is generally, and in this case overwhelmingly, confirmed.

FIG. 70

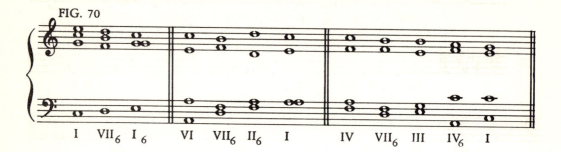

I VII₆ I₆   VI VII₆ II₆ I   IV VII₆ III IV₆ I

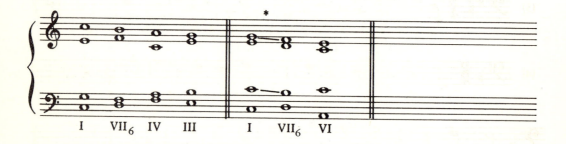

I VII₆ IV III   I VII₆ VI

* A perfect fifth may be followed, stepwise, by a diminished fifth, except when the bass is involved.

Exercises

Figures only.

1. E I–I₆–II₆–V–VI–VII₆–I₆–IV₆–V–I

2. B♭ I–V₆–VII₆–I₆–II₆–V–I

3. A V₆–I–IV₆–VII–III₆–VI–IV–V–I

4. E♭ I–IV₆–III–II₆–VI–V–I

5. D I–VII₆–I₆–I–VI–V–III–II–VII₆–I

6. A♭ I–II₆–I₆–VII₆–VI–III₆–II₆–IV₆–V–I

7. G I₆–VII₆–I–III₆–IV₆–V₆–VI₆–II–V–I

8. D♭ III₆–VI–IV–I–II–I₆–III₆–IV₆–II₆–V–I

9. B I₆–III₆–VI₆–V₆–I–IV₆–I₆–IV–V–I

10. F I–II–VI–III₆–IV–I₆–IV₆–II₆–VII₆–I

Figured basses.

Soprano voice, with chords indicated.

(In the following exercises, in addition to the doublings already allowed, the third may be doubled in six-chords at the points starred. This is always of good effect when smoother or more natural voice leading is thereby made possible. When the doubled third appears in the soprano voice, however, it is to be used with far greater caution than in the case of doubling in the alto or tenor: the third should be doubled in the soprano only on unaccented beats where the movement of the soprano voice, both to and from the tone in question, is stepwise, and where the doubled tone is not higher than both the preceding and following tones.)

* Third to be doubled.

Soprano voice, no chords indicated.

6. SECONDARY TRIADS AND SIX–CHORDS IN THE MINOR MODE

Essential nature of the minor mode

At this point it is necessary to examine more closely the essential nature of the minor mode, its character, and the resources which it contributes. Conventional theory has conceived two forms of the minor scale: the so-called "harmonic" and "melodic" minor scales. In addition to these forms the "natural" or "pure" minor scale (Fig. 14) is sometimes recognized, more often, however, as an abstraction or as a historical survival than otherwise. The term "pure" is preferred here in order to avoid any confusion which may seem to be implied in the term "natural." The latter, in this connection, signifies "unaltered," but the author feels that in speaking of such things as scales or chords any implied — even though not intentional — reference to "Nature" may cause a theoretical confusion (cf. p. 6) which it is better to avoid; in artistic matters it is the human or psychological category of Nature, not physical Nature, that counts.

The difficulty of laying down precise principles regarding the use of the minor mode centers primarily around the question of the raised seventh degree and, to a lesser extent, the raised sixth. The harmonic minor scale represents an attempt to standardize procedure, for theoretical and pedagogical purposes at least, by regarding the seventh degree as always raised and the sixth degree as always minor. It is called "harmonic" because it includes the notes present in the simplest and most frequently found form of the cadence IV–V–I. It is, however, open to obvious objections. Principal among these is the fact that musical practice for over four hundred years has found the interval of the augmented second, which occurs between the sixth and seventh degrees of the harmonic minor scale, awkward and problematical, and has tended consistently to avoid it. Though it is used fairly frequently by the classic composers, it may be said in a general way that this is always done with specific expressive intent.

In the melodic minor scale (see p. 62), both the sixth and the seventh degrees are raised when the scale ascends, and are left unaltered in the descending scale. Undeniably this procedure corresponds far more closely than that of the harmonic minor scale to actual practice. It also gives theoretical recognition to the original purpose of the alterations, which was simply that of providing the tension which is inherent in the character of the leading tone, this tension being a result of the interval of a semitone between the seventh degree and the tonic which follows.

As a working basis for the understanding of the minor mode, the melodic minor scale leaves, therefore, very little to be desired.

In spite of this fact, however, we will adopt not the melodic but the pure minor scale as a point of departure. The primary reason for this is that the pure minor scale is the most "minor" of the various forms. In it, the characteristic intervals — the third, the sixth, and the seventh — are, in contrast to the major mode, all minor intervals, and it will be seen in practice that deviations from this form, even though necessary in the interests of musical articulation, tend to lessen the contrast between the major and the minor mode, and to modify the essential character of the latter. For this reason it seems better to regard the alteration of the sixth and seventh degrees as devices adopted in order to meet specific situations — which, be it readily admitted, are to a great extent the rule rather than the exception, but which nevertheless have the effect of modifying the basic character of the minor mode.

In connection with questions of large harmonic design, in all except matters of detail it is the relations within the pure minor mode which have primary validity. Perhaps this may be made clearer by pointing out that, whereas within the key of c minor the dominant chord is far more often than not the *major* triad of G, it is nevertheless the *key* of g minor, not that of G major, which is most closely related to c minor. Such considerations, of course, belong to a later stage in the study of harmony, and especially of composition, but they are of the greatest importance as regards the nature of key and mode, and the musical logic of which these conceptions are a part.

The point of departure for studying the minor mode will therefore be the pure minor scale with its major second, minor third, minor sixth, and minor seventh — the fourth and fifth being perfect as in the major mode. Three of the degrees, first of all the seventh, but also the sixth and even the second, degrees may be altered, but primarily in specific and definable circumstances. In order to make this question clear it is necessary to consider each alteration in turn as it occurs in different harmonies of the key.

The raised seventh degree

The most important alteration of the minor mode is the raised seventh when it occurs as the third of v. Because of the importance of the progression v–I, the third of the dominant chord functions in this chord far more often than not as the leading tone; consequently, the seventh degree must, at least for the present, be raised in the progression v–I even when the seventh moves to some other tone than the tonic.

The same considerations apply, of course, to the progression v₆–I₆, in which the seventh will generally, and for the present should always, be raised, e.g.:

FIG. 71

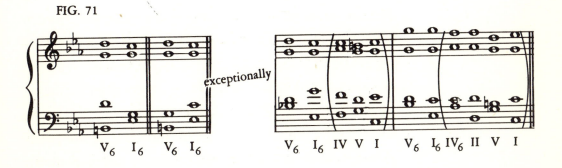

exceptionally

V₆ I₆ V₆ I₆   V₆ I₆ IV V I   V₆ I₆ IV₆ II V I

In the progression V–VI, the seventh degree will be raised in every case of a deceptive cadence (p. 86), and also in most other cases. In this progression the raised seventh must always move to the tonic even though this means doubling the third in VI. Very occasionally, when the succession V–VI is an incidental part of a longer harmonic progression, the seventh degree may be left unaltered.

In the progression V_6–VI, the seventh degree will, of course, be unaltered, and in V_6–VI_6 it will be altered.

FIG. 72

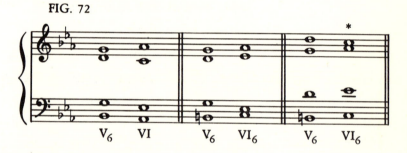

V_6 VI V_6 VI_6 V_6 VI_6

* Third doubled to avoid consecutive fifths.

In the progression V–IV, it may be assumed for present purposes that the seventh degree is always to be raised and that it must always move one degree upward to the tonic.

In the progression V_6–IV, the seventh degree will, provisionally, be altered if the bass rises, unaltered if it falls, although later experience will modify this usage; in V_6–IV_6 the seventh degree will be unaltered, regardless of whether or not the sixth degree in IV_6 is altered.

In the progression V–II the seventh degree will not move to the tonic, which is not present in the triad of II. Aside from the (for purposes of study only) hard and fast rule that the augmented second must always be avoided, it is impossible to lay down inviolable principles concerning alterations in such progressions. The seventh degree will, however, be most often altered when it progresses upward, and left unaltered when it progresses downward. The determining factor will eventually be the context and the sense of the progression as a whole; only an attentive ear, and a certain experience, can be of use here.

In the progression v_6–ii_6, the seventh degree, for the present, will be altered if the bass rises and unaltered if it falls, though later experience will modify this rule.

FIG. 73

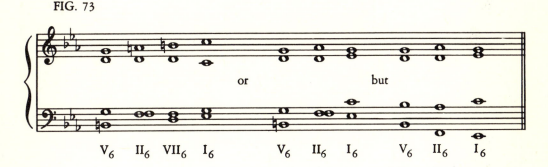

In the progressions v–iii (or iii$_6$) and v–vii (or vii$_6$), the seventh degree occurs in both chords, and the question of alteration will depend on the ultimate destination of the note. Both chromatic progressions and cross relations (see p. 290) are, for the present, to be completely avoided.

FIG. 74

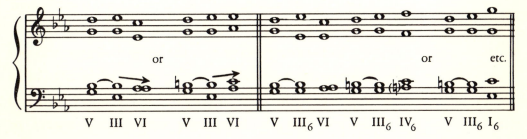

III with the unaltered seventh degree, the chord of the so-called "relative major," is the triad on the most characteristically "minor" degree in the minor mode, and, for that reason, usage has given it much greater importance than the mediant harmony in the major mode. The raised fifth (i.e., the seventh degree of the scale) changes it to an "augmented" triad — major third, augmented fifth — and hence a dissonance. Use of this augmented triad, however, presents no problems except that of the immediate or eventual resolution of the raised seventh. In the case of III as in all other chords containing the seventh degree, the unaltered seventh is never to be moved to the tonic.

FIG. 75

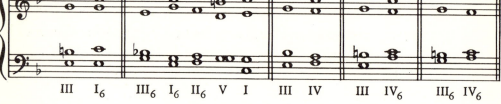

In the case of VII, the diminished triad on the raised root will be very seldom used. Since according to the principles already laid down (p. 75) in connection with the major mode, it must resolve to the augmented triad, and since the root — an altered tone — can under no circumstances be doubled, the resulting voice progression is awkward in the progression VII–III, though not in the progression VII–III₆.

FIG. 76

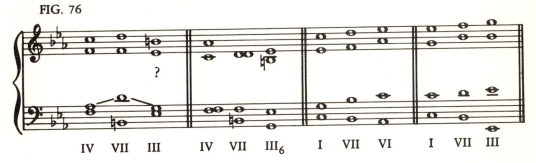

IV VII III   IV VII III₆   I VII VI   I VII III

VII₆, however, is used in the minor as well as in the major mode without restrictions, and the root will be raised or not, according to the principles already established.

FIG. 77

I VII₆ I₆   I VII₆ IV₆ IV   I VII₆ VI₆ V₆

The raised sixth degree

The alteration of the sixth degree is strictly subordinate to that of the seventh degree and, be it once more emphasized, has for its purpose only the avoidance of the augmented second formed between an unaltered sixth degree and a raised seventh degree. Alteration of the sixth degree depends strictly on the voice leading. It may be said in general, however, that, since the unaltered sixth degree is one of the most characteristic features of the minor mode, care should be taken to avoid a too constant use of progressions which involve the substitution for it of the altered tone. The best normal usage will be achieved if the raised sixth is considered as the exception rather than the rule — an exception which, to be sure, contributes not only increased flexibility in the treatment of the minor mode, but added resources to the harmonic vocabulary. It will be seen readily that with the sixth and seventh degrees raised, II, IV, V, and VII become identical with the corresponding chords in the major mode, and that exclusive use of such altered chords, even in short passages, can easily destroy the character of the minor. It will be seen later that this very fact may eventually become a musical resource rather than a disadvantage. But for the present the object is to gain as much ease and resourcefulness as possible within the limits of the minor mode itself, and therefore all that tends to be uncharacteristic should be used with great caution.

II with the fifth raised is transformed from a diminished to a minor triad. While the diminished triad II in its fundamental position will proceed only to V, according to principles already studied in connection with VII in both modes (pp. 75, 110), the minor triad II#5 may also proceed to V, but with different voice leading:

FIG. 78

II altered may, of course, also proceed to III and VII:

FIG. 79

The raised sixth degree in VI changes the chord from a major to a diminished triad; since this would entail a resolution to II, and since holding the altered tone would

IV with the third raised is transformed from a minor to a major triad. It will be seen that in all the possible progressions both alternatives are possible.

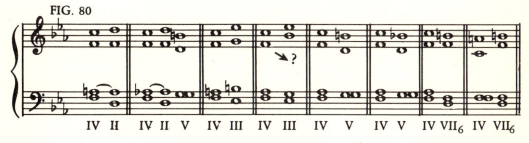

FIG. 80

In the progressions IV₆–V₆ and IV₆–VII both the sixth and the seventh degrees must always, for the present, be raised. In the progressions IV₆–III, IV₆–III₆, IV₆–V, and IV₆–VI, the third of IV₆ will remain unaltered.

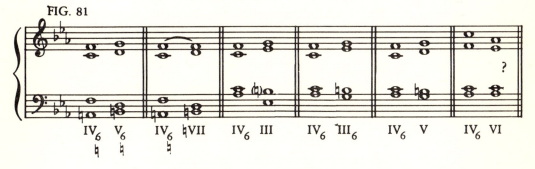

FIG. 81

The raised sixth degree in VI changes the chord from a major to a diminished triad; since this would entail a resolution to II, and since holding the altered tone would involve the use of II_4^6, the use of altered VI must be deferred until six-four chords are considered in detail (Chapter Five).

Altered VI_6, however, may be used like any other six-chord, provided the altered note is never doubled and is always held over or moved directly to the altered seventh degree.

FIG. 82

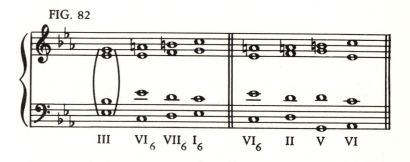

III VI_6 VII_6 I_6 VI_6 II   V   VI

The minor second degree

Any complete consideration of the minor mode must take account of one other alteration which, while not adopted for reasons of structure or articulation, is a part of the common usage of the minor mode. This alteration involves lowering the second degree a half step in II and thus converting that chord from a diminished to a major triad. This alteration occurs generally in the progression II_6–V–I and the resulting $\flat\text{II}_6$ chord is frequently called the "Neapolitan Sixth," after the so-called "Neapolitan School" of composers who at one time were credited with its first general usage. It will be seen that the lowered second degree commonly progresses downward, either to the leading tone, with which it forms the characteristic interval of a diminished third, or to an intermediate tonic note which then proceeds to the leading tone.

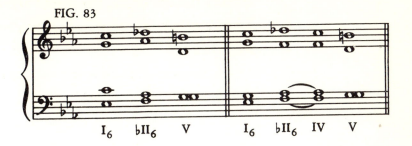

FIG. 83

$$I_6 \quad \flat II_6 \quad V \qquad I_6 \quad \flat II_6 \quad IV \quad V$$

The second degree is also frequently lowered in the fundamental position (also, as will be seen later, in II_4^6) and hence is sometimes called the "Phrygian Second" in allusion to the medieval Phrygian Mode.

FIG. 84

$$VI \quad \flat II \quad V \quad I$$

While the lowered second degree is also used occasionally in chords other than II, these usages belong rather under the heading of chromatic alteration, a topic which must be left for later consideration (Chapters Eight, Ten, and Twelve).

In summary, it will be seen that each degree of the minor mode, with the exception of the tonic, allows at least two forms of the triad, while II has three possibilities in general use:

FIG. 85

While the resources of the minor mode are thus seen to be greater than those of the major mode, it should be clear that these resources involve much greater problems. All of the above considerations (pp. 104–115) should, therefore, be carefully studied and constantly kept in mind while working out the following exercises.

Exercises

Figures only.

1. d $I-IV-VII-III-VI-II-V_\sharp-I$

2. e $I-V-VI-III-IV-V_\sharp^6-I-IV_6-V_\sharp-I$

3. e♭ $I-VII-VI-II_6-III-IV-{}^\natural VII_6-I_6-IV_\natural-VII_{\natural 6}-I$

4. a $I-VI-II-V_\sharp-IV_6-III_{\sharp 5}-VI-{}^\flat II-V_\sharp-I$

5. f $I-II_6-III_{\natural 5}-VI-VII_{\natural 6}-I-{}^\flat II_6-V_\natural-I$

6. b $I-V_6-IV_6-II_6-V_6-VI-IV-V_\sharp-I$

7. g♯ $I-III_{\times 5}-II_{\sharp 5}-V_{\times}-VI-I_6-{}^\natural II_6-V_{\times}-I$

8. c $I-VI-II_6-V_\natural-IV_\natural^6-V_\natural^6-I-{}^\flat II_6-V_\natural-I$

9. f♯ $I-III_{\sharp 5}-IV_6-V_\sharp^{6*}-VI_{\sharp 6}-VII_{\sharp 6}-I_6-VI-{}^\natural II-V_\sharp-I$

10. b♭ $I-V_\natural^6-I_6-II_6-III_\natural^6-VI_6-III-{}^\flat II_6-V_\natural-I$

* Skip of diminished seventh in the bass between third and fourth chord.

Exercises without alterations indicated. The alterations should be, of course, carried out in a correct manner, but it will be found that in some cases a choice of alternatives is possible.

11. c♯ $I-II-V-VI-III-II-V_6-IV_6-II_6-V-I$

12. g $I-V-III-IV_6-II_6-III_6-I_6-II-V-I$

13. d♯ $I-VI_6-V_6-IV_6-II-I_6-V_6-I$

14. a♭ $I-III_6-IV_6-V_6-VI_6-V-VI-I_6-IV-I$

15. e $I-VII_6-III-VI-II_6-V-I_6-II-VI-V-I$

Figured basses.

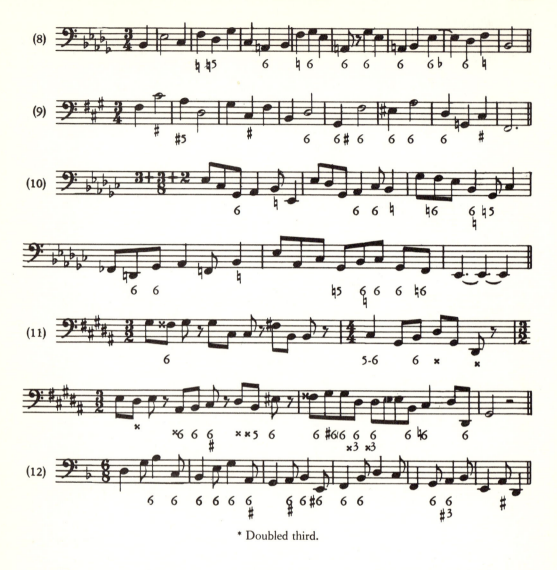

* Doubled third.

Soprano voice, with chords indicated.

* A skip of a diminished seventh in the bass is permissible here.

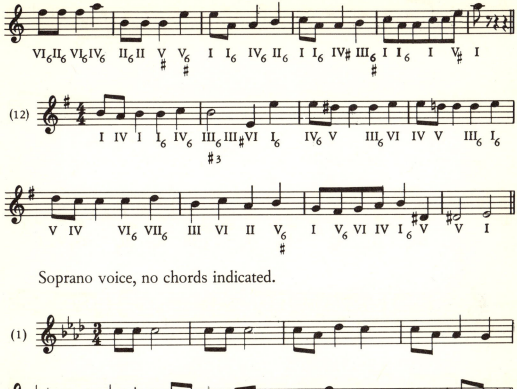

VI₆ II₆ VI₆ IV₆ II₆ II V♯ V₆ I I₆ IV₆ II₆ I I₆ IV♯ III₆ I I₆ I V♯ I

(12) I IV I I₆ IV₆ III₆ III♯ VI I₆   IV₆ V   III₆ VI IV V   III₆ I₆
                    ♯3

V IV VI₆ VII₆ III VI II V₆ I V₆ VI IV I₆ V ♯V I
                          ♯

Soprano voice, no chords indicated.

(1)

(2)

(3)

(4)

(5)

(6)

(7)

(8)

Same — both major and minor.

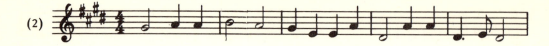

CHAPTER

FIVE

Introduction to Dissonance

1. ACCESSORY TONES

Accessory tones may, for present purposes, be described as tones which do not belong to the chords used, but are introduced for the purpose of gaining a more flowing, more ornate, or more expressive melodic line or texture, or of supplying movement at points where it is required, but not furnished by the chords themselves. This describes accessory tones, of course, from the strictly chordal point of view; actually they belong primarily to the sphere of melody and counterpoint rather than that of harmony, and should from the first be recognized as essential musical elements and not as mere embellishments of a harmonic design. They are by definition dissonant (pp. 14 ff.), and in fact the use of dissonance even as practiced today may be traced in part to the gradually more extended use of accessory tones in connection with otherwise consonant harmony. This statement may seem to be contradicted by the fact that much contemporary music which uses dissonances with apparently complete freedom finds its principle in a polyphony which seems to have freed itself completely from harmonic considerations. But it must be pointed out that this development has taken place in the wake of a long period in which the boldest combinations were developed for quite other than strictly polyphonic purposes.

The study of accessory tones may therefore be considered as the first step in the study of dissonance as such. From this point on, all dissonant chords, even when they have been systematized and classified by harmonic theory (see Chapter Six, "Seventh Chords"), will be treated with reference to this point of view. Although the diminished and augmented triads belong to the same general category, they have been introduced previous to this point for the sake of completeness, and in order to reduce theoretical discussion to the smallest degree compatible with an adequate presentation of the material.

The following classifications represent, so to speak, the fundamental types of accessory tones; from these types, all the freer usages are derived. It will be seen fairly early that only the most basic types can be classified, and that a point is rapidly reached where minute classification and terminology are impossible.

The terminology given here is in general use, although the term "neighboring tone" is more variously applied than the others — its use in the following limited connection being therefore somewhat arbitrary. Far more important than terminology, however, is an understanding, which can be gained only through practice and experience, of the nature and possibilities of these fundamental accessory-tone types, which may be classified in two general groups: the "*unaccented*" and the "*accented*." *It should be clearly understood that the terms "unaccented" and "accented" refer here simply to the position of the accessory tone with relation to the tones which immediately precede and follow it.* Thus, a typically accented accessory tone may occur on a weak beat provided a consonance follows before the next stronger beat. Likewise, a normally unaccented type may be used on a strong beat provided that the preceding and following tones are still stronger with respect to the phrase as a whole, or provided that the purely transitional or ornamental character of the tone is quite clear. Examples:

FIG. 86

C I I₆ V VI III VI IV VII₆ I₆ II₆ I

* Indicates accented accessory tone occurring on a weak beat.

FIG. 87

I VI I₆ IV I V VI ♭II V♯ I

* Indicates unaccented accessory tone occurring on a strong beat.

Accessory tones may be introduced at any time into

any of the voices, but care should be taken to use them — like everything else — only when a definite musical purpose is served. It should also be noted that excessive use of accessory tones can easily lead to an overloading of the texture.

Unaccented accessory tones

1. A *"passing tone"* fills the space between two different tones, which lie in the same voice, by diatonic stepwise motion.

FIG. 88

VI   IV   I   I₆   V   I   I   I₆ V   V₆

I   IV   I I₆ VII₆   VI   I   V₆   II₆

* Passing tone.

2. A *"neighboring tone"* (or "auxiliary tone") is an unaccented tone one step above or below a harmonic tone, which returns immediately to the same tone.

FIG. 89

* Neighboring tone.

3. An "*anticipation*" is a tone which anticipates on a weak beat the note to which the voice in question is moving on the following strong beat.

FIG. 90

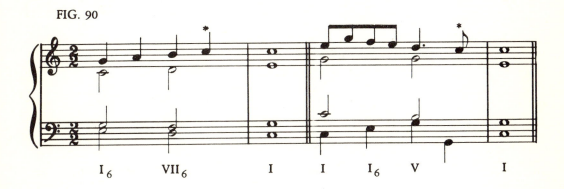

V_6 I I_6 V IV_6 II VII_6 III I_6 IV_6 V   I

* Anticipation.

In a general sense the passing tone is *transitional;* the neighboring tone and the anticipation are *ornamental* or *expressive,* in character and origin. While it is impossible to establish rules in this respect, the latter types, especially the anticipation, can easily be abused, and require more care if they are to be used to good effect.

Accented accessory tones

1. A *"suspension"* is a tone held over from one chord (*"preparation"*) to the next one, with which it forms a dissonance (the suspension proper); the latter resolves by moving one step downward or upward to a chord tone (*"resolution"*). The following should be observed:

a) Downward resolution is more usual, but upward resolution (Fig. 91 (b)) is possible if the interval of resolution is a semitone.

b) The suspension must be no longer than the preparation (Fig. 91 (c)).

c) The resolution must take place on a beat or beat division which is metrically weaker than that of the suspension proper (Fig. 91 (d)).

d) The resolution should not result in a doubled third or fifth, nor should the preparation and resolution form consecutive fifths or octaves with other voices (Fig. 91 (e) and (f)).

FIG. 91 (a)

I   II₆   I₆   V   I   I₆   VII₆

VI₆   V₆   I   I   III   IV₆   I   II   I₆   II₆   V   I

(b)   *(c)*   *(d)*

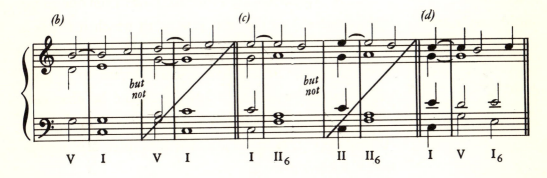

V   I   V   I   I   II₆   II   II₆   I   V   I₆

(e)   *(f)*

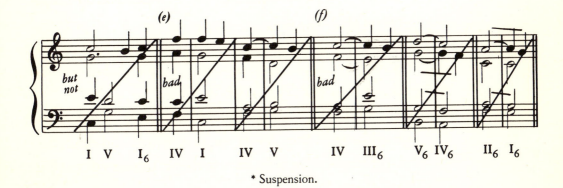

I   V   I₆   IV   I   IV   V   IV   III₆   V₆   IV₆   II₆   I₆

* Suspension.

2. An *"appoggiatura"* is, so to speak, a suspension without preparation — i.e., an accented dissonance which resolves stepwise, within the harmony, on a weaker beat or beat division.

IV   I   I₆   IV   V₆   I   IV   II   V
(II₆-IV)

I   II   V₆   I   III   VI   II   V   I

V   I₆   IV₆   VI
(III₆ V)

* Appoggiatura.

Generally speaking, the tone of resolution of a suspension or an appoggiatura should not double a tone
already present in the chord, e.g.:

If the appoggiatura is lower than the doubled tone, e.g.:

this is still more definitely to be avoided.

Exceptions may be allowed in the first of these cases
(appoggiatura in an upper voice), provided the doubled
tone is not the leading tone; in the second case (appoggiatura in the lower voice), only if the doubled tone is
the tonic; e.g.:

Exercises

Soprano voice, with chords indicated.

(2)

I   IV   V   VI   IV₆   IV   V   V₆

I   IV   III₆   VI IV I   IV₆   II₆   V   I

(3)

I   VI   II   V₆   I   IV₆ IV   I₆ VI V

I   IV₆   VII₆   III₆   IV   I₆   I   V   I

(4)

I   VII₆   I₆   V₆   II₆   VII₆ I₆ I   II₆ IV₆ V

II₆   I₆   V₆   I   II₆   IV₆   I₆   V   I

(5)

I   II₆   I₆ II   III₆   II₆ III   II₇₋₆ I   I₆   VII₆   I   V₆

I₆   VII₆ I   VI I   V   VI   IV₆ V₆   I   I₆ IV   V₈₋₇ I

(6)

I   V₆   I₆   VI   VII₆ III₆   IV₆   V₆ V V₆ I   VI   IV

I₆   II   VI   IV₆   II₆   VI   VII₆   III₆   I₆   I   IV₆   I₆ I₆ V   I

(7) I V₆ IV₆ I V VI I₆ IV₆

I I₆ VII₆ II₆ III VI II₆ II V I

(8) I V₆ I I₆ IV IV₆ VII VII₆

III VI₆ VII₆ IV V V₆ VI IV V I

(9) I II₆ II VI IV I₆ V IV₆ IV I₆ II III₆ III

VII₆ I₆ IV II V V₆ II V₆ I₆ VI II II₆ V

(10) I IV V I IV₆ IV V I VI VI₆

III₆ II₆ I₆ VII₆ I V IV II₆ V

IV II₆ V IV IV₆ I I₆ II₆ IV V I

(11) I V₆ I III IV V III IV V₆ VII₆ I IV₆ V III₆ III IV

II₆ VII III   III₆ VI₆ VII₆   III₆   II₆   III   I₆ VI   I₆ II₆   V   I

(12) I   IV₆   I   II₆   I₆   IV₆   I   I   V   I₆   V   III₆

I₆ IV   V   VII₆   VI   II₆   II   VI   II   IV₆   V   I

* Accessory tone.

Soprano voice, no chords indicated. The asterisks, indicating accessory tones, are to be taken merely as suggestions, not necessarily binding, for the help of the student.

(1)

(2)

(3)

(4)

(5)

(6)

(7)

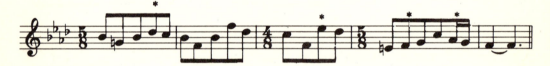

(8)

(9)

* Accessory tone.

Soprano voice, no chords or accessory tones indicated.

Moderato

Andante

Molto vivace

Moderato

(4)

Andante

(5)

Allegretto

(6)

Presto

(7)

Allegro moderato

(8)

2. THE SIX-FOUR CHORD

The six-four chord — the "second inversion" of the triad, with the fifth in the lowest voice:

FIG. 93

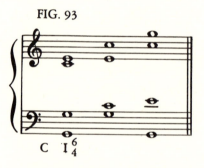

derives its special character from its interval of a fourth, of which the effect is discussed on page 16. It has very seldom the sense of an independent chord; if it acquires this sense, it is practically always due to exceptional situations in the leading of the bass voice. Thus, in (a) below (both examples), the fifth (bass) and the third (soprano) of the six-four chord are passing tones; in (b), the fifth is a neighboring tone, while the third is a passing tone. In (c) the root and the third of the chord are essentially appoggiaturas.

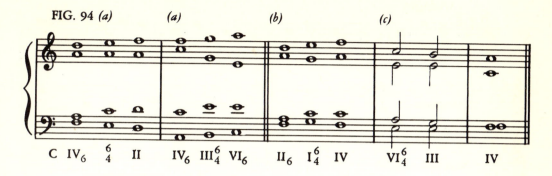

$$\text{C} \quad \text{IV}_6 \quad {}^6_4 \quad \text{II} \qquad \text{IV}_6 \quad \text{III}^6_4 \quad \text{VI}_6 \qquad \text{II}_6 \quad \text{I}^6_4 \quad \text{IV} \qquad \text{VI}^6_4 \quad \text{III} \qquad \text{IV}$$

While the above covers completely the sense of the six-four chord when used in this manner, the actual usage is somewhat freer, and, in the upper voices (i.e., all voices except the bass), not subject to the restrictions which have been thus far applied to accessory tones (pp. 127 ff.). However, the bass must either be approached stepwise or held over from the preceding chord; it must also either be held over or proceed stepwise to the bass of the next chord (see Fig. 95, below).

FIG. 95

$$\text{IV}_6 \quad \text{II}^6_4 \quad \text{III}_6 \qquad \text{I} \quad \text{VI}^6_4 \quad \text{VII}_6 \qquad \text{IV} \quad \text{I}^6_4 \quad \text{IV}_6 \qquad \text{V} \quad \text{I}^6_4 \quad \text{IV}_6$$

While the six-four chord is nearly always accessory in character and only rarely of essential harmonic importance, it may still be considered as rhythmically equivalent to other chords, with the single reservation that, of course, it will certainly not for the present, and only most exceptionally in any case, be possible to begin or end a phrase with it. The student cannot go far wrong in using it if he regards its figuration as purely formal, and considers it as in no sense the equivalent of the triad of which it is, in the purely literal sense, an inversion.

Extension of the six-four chord in the cadence

A much more frequent usage of the six-four chord occurs in a very common cadence formula, in which the root and the third of I_4^6 are in reality appoggiaturas or suspensions which resolve respectively to the third and the fifth of the dominant chord following:

FIG. 96

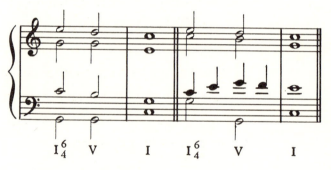

The so-called tonic six-four chord is here in reality a part of the dominant harmony, and makes possible the extension of the latter harmony.

(N.B. The above-mentioned process of extension is one which contains vast implications for musical rhythm and movement, and which will come into greater and greater consideration as the study of harmony proceeds. Its nature may be graphically illustrated in the "*cadenza*" (the Italian word for "cadence") of the classic concerto. The cadenza is introduced by a *fermata* in the orchestra on the tonic six-four chord. After the six-four chord is broken off the soloist is permitted to improvise freely and

at length, with no harmonic restrictions whatever except
the necessity of closing his improvisation on the third or
the fifth of the dominant chord, thus resolving the original six-four chord; the orchestra then enters on the tonic.
The point is that the tension or psychological suspense
created by the six-four chord persists in the mind of the
hearer and allows even a very extended interruption in
the development of the basic harmonic flow. The following examples are quoted literally from several classic con-
certos.)

FIG. 97

BEETHOVEN, *Violin Concerto* (Op. 51)

BEETHOVEN, *Piano Concerto No. 4 (Op. 58)*

MOZART, *Piano Concerto in C Minor* (K. 491)

The extension or elaboration of harmonies (see pp.
200 ff.) is one of the principal means through which large

musical forms are created, and the above gives only the barest hint of a practically unlimited subject. The usage in cadenzas of the I_4^6 chord is, however, an excellent point of departure for its study.

Position and treatment of the six-four chord

A I_4^6 chord will always, for the present, be accented relatively to a dominant chord into which it resolves. The same formula of resolution may, of course, be carried out on any other degree of the scale — i.e., II_4^6–VI, IV_4^6–I, etc.:

FIG. 98

I_6 VII_4^6 IV I_4^6 V I I I_6 II_4^6 VI IV V I

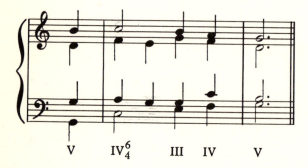

V IV_4^6 III IV V

It must be remembered that when the six-four chord functions as a double appoggiatura or suspension it is the bass — i.e., the fifth and not the root — which is the effective harmonic tone; it is therefore this tone which should be doubled in preference to the root or third. (This does not, however, apply in the case of a six-four chord used as a passing or neighboring harmony, in which case either the fifth or the root, less frequently the third, may be doubled.)

The six-four chord which "resolves" in this manner always carries with it the sense of an accent. If, as in the following

the six-four occurs on a relatively unaccented beat, the effect will be that of a syncopation

or, in the following

of a "delayed" or prolonged resolution.

Exercises

Bar lines indicated. Accessory tones may be introduced in any voice.

1. D: $\frac{2}{2}$ I V$_6$ | II$_4^6$ VI | I$_4^6$ IV | I$_6$ IV$_6$ | I$_4^6$ V | I ‖

2. c: $\frac{3}{4}$ ⸮ I V$_6$ | IV$_6$ I$_4^6$ IV | I$_6$ VII$_6$ I | ♭II$_6$ I$_4^6$ V | I ‖

3. A♭

8. c♯ 4/4
I III | VII$^6_4$ I$_6$ V$^6_4$ | I IV$_6$ I$_6$ II$_6$ | I$^6_4$ V | II$^6_4$ III$^6_4$
VI$_6$ II$_6$ III$_6$ | II$^6_4$ IV$_6$ I$^6_4$ V | I IV$^6_4$ I
9. D♭ 3/4
I | IV$^6_4$ III$^6_4$ IV$_6$ VI | II$^6_4$ I$^6_4$ IV II$_6$ | I$_6$ II$_6$ V I$_6$ VII$_6$ | I I$_6$ V I
I I$^6_4$ I$^6_4$ II$^6_4$ II$^6_4$ V$_6$ | IV$^6_4$ I VI IV$^6_4$ I | VII$^6_4$ IV I$^6_4$ VI II$_6$ V | IV$^6_4$ I
10. f 6/8
I V$^6_4$ I$_6$ ♭II$_6$ I$^6_4$ VII$^6_4$ | I$_6$ VII$_6$ III II$_6$ | I$^6_4$ II$^6_4$ I$^6_4$ II$_6$ I$^6_4$ V
I IV$^6_4$ I V I | (♭)VII I VII III ♭II$_6$ | VI ♭II VI III(♮)
VI III VI II$_6$ I$_6$ | V$^6_4$ VII$_6$ I$_6$ II$^6_4$ VI ♭II | I$^6_4$ V VI IV II$_6$ V | I

Soprano voice, with chords indicated.

* I.e., II₆ with ninth added. See Chapter Seven, "Frozen Accessory Tones" (pp. 224 ff.).

III VII$_6$ V VII$_4^6$I$_6$ I II$_6$ II VII III$_6$ VI I$_6$ V$_{(4\underline{\quad}3)}$ I

(4)

I V$_6$ IV$_6$ I$_4^6$ II$_6$ V I$_6$ VI II

V I$_6$ IV I$_4^6$ II$_4^6$ V$_6$ I$_6$ VII$_6$ I I$_6$ IV$_6$ II I$_4^6$ V I

(5)

I IV$_4^6$ V$_6$ (II$_4^6$)IV VI I$_4^6$ II$_6$ VI$_4^6$II I$_4^6$ V VI III$_6$

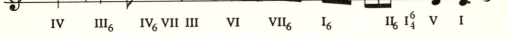

IV III$_6$ IV$_6$ VII III VI VII$_6$ I$_6$ II$_6$ I$_4^6$ V I

(6)

V IV II$_6$ V IV V ♭II$_4^6$VI ♭II V III IV IV$_6$ II$_6$

V III$_6$I$_6$ IV$_6$ I$_6$ IV$_6$ III$_6$ I IV$_6$ I$_4^6$ V(III$_6$) I

Soprano voice, no chords indicated.

Semplice

(1)

Andantino

(2)

Tempo di menuetto

(3)

Andante

(4)

CHAPTER

SIX

Seventh Chords
and Their Inversions

Up to this point, the chords studied — whether dissonant or not — have all been derived from the triad. That is to say, they have been chords consisting of three tones, of which the prototype is the major triad and its inversions. In a broad sense, the triads represent the basic harmonic expression of the various degrees of the diatonic scale, and the six-chords — with certain exceptions which will be considered in Chapter Seven (p. 228) — represent alternative weaker forms of these same triads. The six-four chord, as has been indicated, is very seldom used as such a basic harmonic expression, and then only under special circumstances; more generally speaking it is the equivalent of a dissonant chord, and as such is subordinate to the harmonies which precede or follow it, according to the context.

1. STRICTER USE OF SEVENTH CHORDS

The seventh chord is a triad with an added dissonant tone, the seventh. The seventh will of course be either major or minor (see Fig. 99), or diminished (see Fig. 107).

FIG. 99

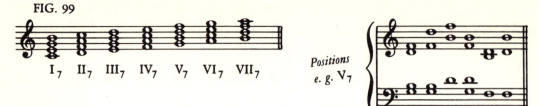

Positions
e. g. V₇

According to a conception which will be further developed later, this added seventh may be considered as an accessory tone which has been, so to speak, frozen on the triad, which thus deprives the latter of its consonant (i.e., its "stable" or "conclusive") character, and which, most often, leads down one step to a tone in the following chord. In the preliminary exercises, the seventh chord must be treated in the strict manner familiar already in connection with the treatment of the diminished triad (as outlined on page 75). That is, the dissonance — in this case, the seventh — must be "prepared" or held over from the preceding chord, and must "resolve" by moving one step downward to the third of the following chord, which will, for the present, be in the relationship of the lower fifth with respect to the seventh chord in question. The following examples will make this clear:

FIG. 100

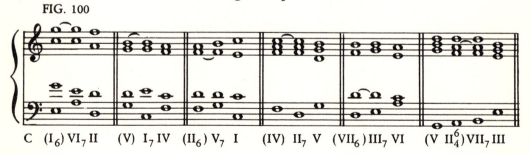

C (I₆) VI₇ II   (V) I₇ IV   (II₆) V₇ I   (IV) II₇ V   (VII₆) III₇ VI   (V II₄⁶) VII₇ III

Since, in the diatonic scales as thus far studied, the seventh chords show a variety of structure, sometimes resulting in special problems of voice leading, it will be found helpful to group them in various categories as follows:

1. Most seventh chords which are derived from major and minor triads, and in which the seventh is unaltered, may be considered together, in spite of differences in structure. These include, in the major mode, I₇, IV₇ (in which a major seventh is added to a major triad); II₇, III₇, and VI₇ (in which a minor seventh is added to a minor triad); in the minor mode they include the corresponding chords III₇, VI₇, IV₇, V₇, and I₇, all unaltered. In the case of these two chord types, preparation and resolution present no problems.

FIG. 101

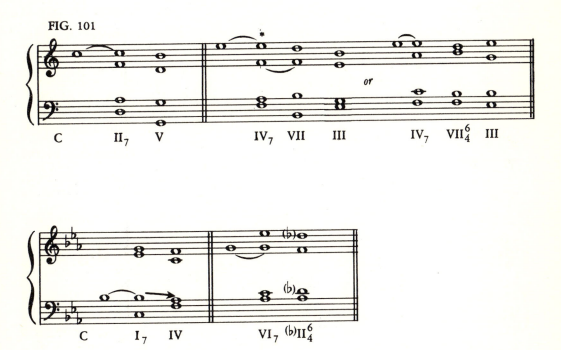

* The fifth of VII must be prepared; therefore the root of IV₇ must be doubled, and the fifth omitted.

The resolution to the six-chord is seldom good, as it produces a direct octave to the doubled third, e.g.:

2. v_7 in the major, and vII_7 unaltered and v_7 altered in the minor, consist of a minor seventh added to a major triad, thus forming a diminished fifth between the third and seventh of the chord. In the case of vII_7 in the minor this presents no problems, the resolution being the same as in the chords listed under (1). In the case of the two dominant seventh chords, however, the third is the leading tone and as such must be treated with a certain care. It should be taken to the tonic note whenever it lies in the soprano voice, thus necessitating either the tripling of the root in the tonic chord (see (c) below), or the omission of the fifth and doubling of the root of the dominant seventh (see (b) below). But if the third lies in one of the middle voices, the chord may be resolved in the same manner as those listed under (1) (see (a) below).

FIG. 102

The dominant seventh chord is by far the most commonly used of all the sevenths, and for this reason it may

even at this point be treated with somewhat more freedom than the other seventh chords. It will therefore not
be necessary to prepare the seventh; the chord may be
introduced freely at any point where the dominant harmony is called for, with one exception — since the chord
must still be resolved, it will obviously not be suitable as
the last chord of a phrase.

The dominant seventh chord may also at this point
resolve to VI, in which case the third will naturally be
doubled in the latter chord, as in the following examples:

FIG. 103

V_7 VI V_7 III V_7 VI

This resolution V_7–VI will be found especially useful
in the deceptive cadence (p. 86). In fact, it will always
have the character, to some extent, of a deceptive cadence,
due to the "pull" of the seventh added to that of the
dominant harmony (see also page 211); for this reason,
it is likely to be followed, after a short interval, by the
progression V_7–I.

Care should always be taken not to overdo the use
of the dominant seventh chord, or to use it where the
ordinary dominant triad is more appropriate — one of
the most frequent mistakes made by beginners in harmony. Like every other dissonance, the dominant seventh
chord contains the element of tension; it is in other words
a chord with a "tendency," and its effect is therefore quite
different from that of the triad. This difference can be

learned only by careful and sensitive observation and experience, but should be kept attentively in mind from the very start.

3. VII$_7$ in the major, and II$_7$ unaltered in the minor, add a minor seventh to a diminished triad, and therefore add the dissonance of the seventh to that of the diminished fifth. Owing to the greater sonority and definition given to it by the seventh, it is this chord, and not the diminished triad, that is by far the more usual harmonic form taken by the seventh degree in actual music. Although for reasons of logic the diminished triad has been discussed earlier (pp. 75, 110–111), it should from now on be considered as a definitely less preferable form of this harmony, to be used only when circumstances of voice leading or other factors make the triad definitely more appropriate, in a given context, than the corresponding seventh chord.

It should also be observed that while the fifth may sometimes be omitted in the seventh chords which contain the perfect fifth, this is not generally acceptable in seventh chords containing a diminished fifth (cf. triads, pp. 53, 75). The fifth, like the third and seventh, is an essential ingredient of the latter chords, and must always be present.

For the present, it is necessary to prepare and resolve not only the seventh but the fifth as well. It will be found, however, that this does not in any way restrict the use of the chord, since the harmonies which have been available in preparing the fifth of the diminished triad (II and IV in major and IV and VI in minor) contain the seventh as well, and this seventh will resolve naturally to the third of the chord of resolution (III in major and V in minor).

FIG. 104

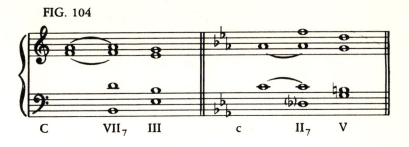

4. The seventh chords in the minor mode which contain altered notes (with the exception of $v_{7\#}$, already discussed on page 160) raise special problems, since the alterations must, for the present, still be treated in the most strict and logical manner. Thus for instance $II_{\#5}^7$, if resolved according to the above principles, would result in a doubled leading tone; the resolution of $IV_{\#}^7$ would require such forced voice leading that it may be considered for the present as unusable. $\#VI_{7}$, with an altered root, may be resolved to II_4^6, provided the raised tone eventually moves to the raised seventh degree (see pp. 61, 105). $III_{\#5}^7$ results in a doubled third in the chord VI to which it resolves. Examples:

FIG. 105

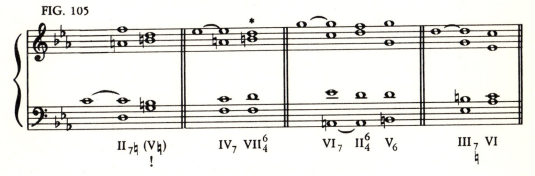

* Only possible resolution at this point.

$I_{\#7}$ and $VII_{\#7}$ are obviously (since the seventh cannot resolve downward) inconsistent with the basic sense of the seventh chord and are not (for the present) to be used. When they occur they are to be interpreted according to principles which have not yet been studied (see Chapter Ten).

FIG. 106

VII

5. #VII₇, with the root raised and the seventh unaltered, belongs in a quite special category, and must be considered separately from the other seventh chords. It is the familiar chord of the diminished seventh, and contains a diminished seventh added to a diminished triad. When used in the strictest manner it may be regarded as the counterpart in the minor mode of VII₇ in the major mode, and the remarks under (3) above could be applied to this chord as well, were it not for the fact that the root, being altered, must remain stationary, resulting in III$^6_4$:

FIG. 107

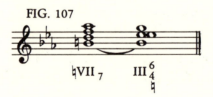

♮VII ₇   III $^6_4$
                ♮

This, however, does not cover even the elementary use of the diminished seventh chord, which has always been treated in a somewhat special way. The real properties of the diminished seventh chord result from the fact that it divides the octave into four equal parts; because of this, it has acquired a large degree of what may be called ambiguity — ambiguity which has been exploited to the full by the composers of the past two hundred years — that is, since the general adoption of the tempered scale.

Since the intervals which make up the chord are equal, the functions of the various tones are not inherent in the diatonic structure of the chord. This fact leads to the rather curious result that, since all the tones are equally dissonant, none of them need be prepared; and since, similarly, all the tones are equal, any one of them can function as a root — i.e., as a *leading tone*. As will be seen later (pp. 363–364), this makes the chord a very easy and in itself not too subtle means of modulation.

For the present, however, the chord must be kept within the key, and its use should be limited to the progressions VII$_7$–I and VII$_7$–III$^6_4$, as follows:

FIG. 108

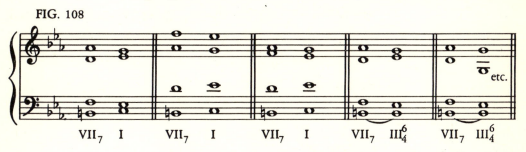

VII$_7$ I   VII$_7$ I   VII$_7$ I   VII$_7$ III$^6_4$ VII$_7$ III$^6_4$

In these above positions the third should be doubled in I, in order to avoid fifths; but in the following positions the root will generally be doubled:

FIG. 109

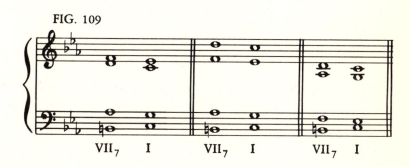

VII$_7$ I   VII$_7$ I   VII$_7$ I

Exercises

Figures only.

1. C I_6–II_7–V–I_7–IV–VII_7–III–VI_7–II–V_7–VI–IV_7–VII_4^6–III_7–VI–V–I

2. e I–IV_7–VII–III_7–VI–II_7–V–I_7–IV–$\natural VII_7$–I–VI_7–II_4^6–V_7–I

3. B I–IV_6–II_7–V–III_7–VI–IV_6–V_7–I

4. d I–IV–V_7–I–$III_{\sharp5}$–VI_7–II_4^6–V_7–I

5. A I–VI_7–II–VII_6–III_7–VI–IV_6–II_7–I_4^6–V–I

6. f I–IV_7–VII–III_7–VI–II_7–V–I

7. E♭ I–IV_7–VII_4^6–I_6–IV_6–II_7–V–III_7–VI_4^6–VII_6–I–VI_7–II–V_7–I

8. c♯ I–VI_7–II–V_7–VI–IV–$III_{\sharp5}$–VI_7–II_4^6–V_7–I_4^6–IV–II_7–V–I

9. G♭ I–V–III_7–VI–IV–VII_7–III–II_6–V–I_7–IV–I_6–VI_7–II–V_7–I

10. b I–VI–II_7–V–III_7–VI–$\natural II_6$–I_4^6–VI_7–II_4^6–III_4^6–I–$\natural II$–V_7–I

11. A♭ I–II–VII_7–III–VI_7–II–V_7–VI–IV_7–VII_4^6–I_6–II_7–V–I_7–IV–V–III_7–VI–V_7–I

12. d♯ I–$III_{\ast5}$–VI_7–$\natural II$–$V_\ast^7$–I_4^6–$II_\sharp^6$–$III_\ast^7$–VI–IV_7–VII–IV_6–V_7–VI–II_7–$V_\ast$–I

2.

THE INVER-SIONS OF THE SEVENTH CHORD

The inversions of the seventh chord: 6–5, 4–3, and 2

FIG. 110

C I_5^6 I_3^4 I_2

require little comment. In the case of all chords except the diminished seventh ($\sharp VII_3^4$ in the minor mode, which resolves to I_6), the 4–3 chord may be resolved to either the triad or the six-chord; the two-chord must resolve to the six-chord, since the seventh is in the bass. The following examples, which are numbered according to the classification of seventh chords on pages 159–165, will make this clear.

FIG. 111 *(1)*

$$I_5^6 \quad IV \qquad I_3^4 \quad IV \qquad I_3^4 \quad IV_6 \qquad I_2 \quad IV_6 \qquad II_5^6 \quad V \qquad II_3^4 \quad V_6 \qquad IV_5^6 \quad VII \text{ etc.}$$

also   but not   etc.   *good*

(2)   (3)   (4)

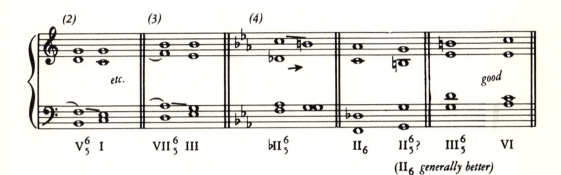

$$V_5^6 \quad I \qquad VII_5^6 \quad III \qquad \flat II_5^6 \qquad II_6 \qquad II_5^6? \quad III_5^6 \quad VI$$

etc.   *good*

(II₆ *generally better*)

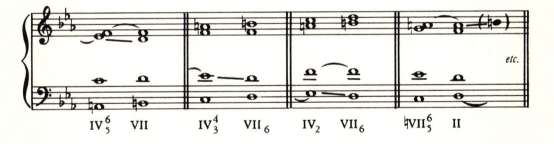

$$IV_5^6 \quad VII \qquad IV_3^4 \quad VII_6 \qquad IV_2 \quad VII_6 \qquad \natural VII_5^6 \quad II$$

etc.

(5)

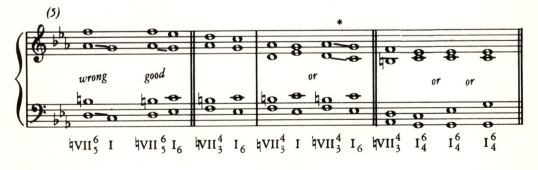

$$\natural VII_5^6 \quad I \qquad \natural VII_5^6 \quad I_6 \qquad \natural VII_3^4 \quad I_6 \qquad \natural VII_3^4 \quad I \qquad \natural VII_3^4 \quad I_6 \qquad \natural VII_3^4 \quad I_4^6 \qquad I_4^6 \qquad I_4^6$$

wrong   good   *or*   *or   or*

* Permissible "fifths."

Just as v_7 is too easily substituted by the beginner for the dominant triad v (p. 161), so v_3^4 is all too frequently

FIG. 112

$$v_3^4 \qquad VII_6$$

used where VII_6 is the stronger chord. The student must learn by observation and practice to distinguish between these chords also, and to use them with discrimination.

Exercises

Figures only.

1. A $I-IV_5^6-VII-III_5^6-VI-II_5^6-V-I_5^6-IV-VII_5^6-III-VI_5^6-II-V_5^6-I$

2. d same chords

3. F♯ $I-IV_3^4-VII-III_3^4-VI-II_3^4-V-I_3^4-IV-VII_3^4-III-VI_3^4-II-$
   v_3^4-I

4. c same chords

5. E♭ $I-II_2-V_6-I_2-IV_6-VII_2-III_6-VI_2-II_6-V_2-I_6-IV_2-VII_6-$
   $III_2-VI_6-II_5^6-V-I$

6. b same chords

7. C♯ $I-II_2-V_6-VI_5^6-II-VII_7-III-IV_3^4-VII_6-I_6-II_3^4-V-I$

8. g $I-IV_4^6-VII_5^{♯6}-I_6-VI_7-♭II-V_5^6-VI_6-II_5^6-V-I$

9. E $I-II_6-VII_5^6-III-I_3^4-IV-V_2-I_6-II_3^4-V-I$

10. b♭ $I-V_3^4-I_6-IV_6-VII_2-III_6-VI_5^6-II-VII_5^{♮6}-I_6-IV-II_3^4-V-I$

11. A♭ $I-VI_7-II_4^6-VII_2-III_6-IV_3^4-VII_6-I_5^6-IV-II_7-V-I$

12. d♯ $I-II_2-V_{\ast}^6-III_{\ast5}^7-VI-II_3^4-V_{\ast}-I_4^6-♯VI_2-II_{\sharp}^6-III_{\ast5}-VI_7-$
    $♮II_4^6-V_7-I$

13. D $I-VI-II_5^6-V-I_7-IV-VII_5^6-III-IV_2-VII_6-I_6-IV_6-I_4^6-V_7-I$

14. g# I_6–※–VII_7–I–VI_7–♮II–V_5^6–I–II_6–III_5^6 –VI_6–II_2–V_6–I_2–
IV_6–$III_※^6$–II_6–V_7–I

Figured basses. Accessory tones may be freely used.

Soprano voice, with chords indicated.

By contrary motion in bass.

3. FREER USE OF SEVENTH CHORDS AND THEIR INVERSIONS

1. Seventh chords may now be introduced without preparation, in the interests of smooth or characteristic voice leading (see (a) and (b) below), or of harmonic force (see (c) and (d) below).

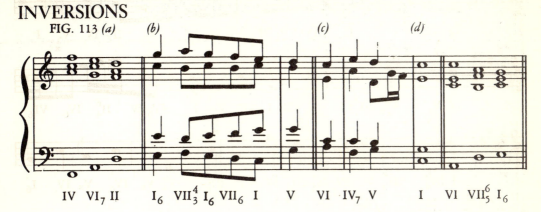

FIG. 113 *(a)*   *(b)*   *(c)*   *(d)*

IV VI₇ II   I₆ VII₃⁴ I₆ VII₆ I   V VI IV₇ V   I VI VII₅⁶ I₆

2. The seventh of the chord may be added to the triad after the latter has been introduced. Once the seventh is present, however, it must remain until the harmony changes; the "empty" triad would seem unsatisfactory after the seventh has been sounded.

FIG. 114

I   I₇ IV   VI VI₇ II   V V₇ I

The addition of the seventh to a triad in such cases, obviously, does not affect the harmonic rhythm, which is always felt in terms of *root progression*, subject only to the qualifications already mentioned on page 79.

3. Seventh chords and their inversions may now

move to chords other than those of the lower fifth, provided that the seventh itself resolves.

FIG. 115

4. Seventh chords and their inversions may move to other seventh chords or inversions of seventh chords, again provided that the seventh is always resolved.

FIG. 116

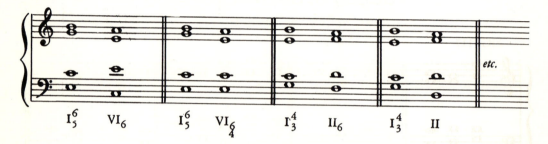

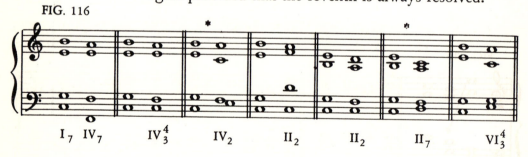

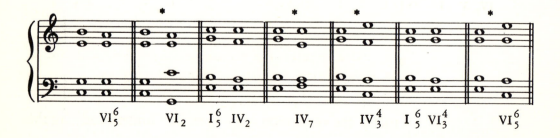

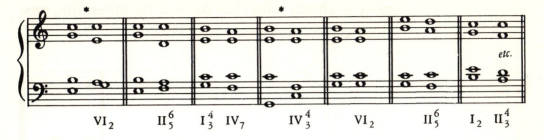

$$VI_2 \quad II_5^6 \quad I_3^4 \ IV_7 \quad IV_3^4 \quad VI_2 \quad II_5^6 \quad I_2 \ II_3^4$$

* Indicates some of the less obvious, but equally logical, possibilities.

5. The position of the seventh chord may be changed, the dissonance shifting from one voice to another, before the resolution (p. 158) takes place.

FIG. 117

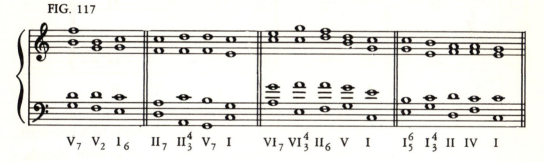

$$V_7 \ V_2 \ I_6 \quad II_7 \ II_3^4 \ V_7 \ I \quad VI_7 \ VI_3^4 \ II_6 \ V \ I \quad I_5^6 \ I_3^4 \ II \ IV \ I$$

6. Finally, the resolution may take place in a voice other than that in which the seventh occurs. And even-

FIG. 118

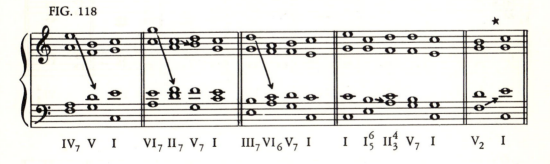

$$IV_7 \ V \ I \quad VI_7 \ II_7 \ V_7 \ I \quad III_7 \ VI_6 \ V_7 \ I \quad I \ I_5^6 \ II_3^4 \ V_7 \ I \quad V_2 \ I$$

* The most drastic case. But compare Bach, *St. John Passion*, Nos. 14, 18, 28, 43, 49, 55 (3 instances), 64, and many other instances.

tually the resolution may even be "understood" as the

omitted fifth of a chord, provided the harmonic sense is clear and the voice leading makes such a procedure desirable. In such cases, however, there is always the danger of too great contrast in sonority; this latter is least likely to occur when the chord of resolution is also a seventh chord.

FIG. 119

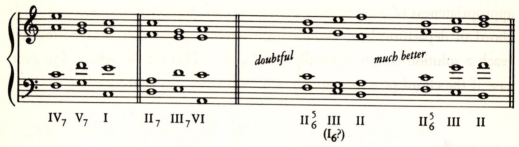

IV_7 V_7 I II_7 III_7 VI II_6^5 III   II II_6^5 III   II
                                                        $(I_6?)$

Exercises

1. $\left.\begin{array}{l} A \\ a \end{array}\right\}$ $I–I_2–II_3^4–VII_2–I_3^4–VI_2–VII_3^4–V_2$, etc. . . . .

2. $\left.\begin{array}{l} E\flat \\ e\flat \end{array}\right\}$ $I–I_7–IV_7–VII_7–III_7–VI_7–II_7$, etc. . . . .

3. $\left.\begin{array}{l} D\flat \\ c\sharp \end{array}\right\}$ $I–I_7–IV_3^4–VII_7–III_3^4–VI_7–II_3^4$, etc. . . . .

4. $\left.\begin{array}{l} B \\ b \end{array}\right\}$ $I–I_7–VI_3^4–VII_7–V_3^4–VI_7–IV_3^4$, etc. . . . .

5. $\left.\begin{array}{l} G \\ g \end{array}\right\}$ $I–VI_5^6–II_2–V_5^6–I_2–IV_5^6–VII_2$, etc. . . . .

6. $\left.\begin{array}{l} E \\ e \end{array}\right\}$ $I–VI_5^6–IV_3^4–V_5^6–III_3^4–IV_5^6$, etc. . . . .

7. $\left.\begin{array}{l} F \\ f \end{array}\right\}$ $I–VI_5^6–IV_5^6–V_5^6–III_5^6–IV_5^6–II_5^6–III_5^6$, etc. . . . .

8. $\left.\begin{array}{l} C \\ c \end{array}\right\}$ $I–VI_3^4–II_3^4–V_3^4–I_3^4–IV_3^4–VII_3^4$, etc. . . . .

9. $\left.\begin{array}{l} F\sharp \\ f\sharp \end{array}\right\}$ $I–VI_3^4–IV_2–V_3^4–III_2–IV_3^4–II_2$, etc. . . . .

10. $\left.\begin{array}{l} D \\ d \end{array}\right\}$ $I-VI_3^4-VII_2-V_3^4-VI_2-IV_3^4-V_2$, etc. ....

11. $\left.\begin{array}{l} Bb \\ bb \end{array}\right\}$ $I-VI_7-VII_2-V_7-VI_2-IV_7-V_2$, etc. ....

In the case of exercises allowing freer use of seventh chords, due note should be taken of the fact that many such progressions result from a contrapuntal rather than a harmonic impulse (see later, pp. 200 ff.), and that the appropriateness of a given progression often depends on the position of the chord of departure. In the following exercises special care must be taken to reach a solution that is musically satisfactory. This can be achieved in every case if the chord positions are chosen with some care and foresight.

12. Eb $\frac{2}{2}$

I | I_3^4 VI | VII_2 I_3^4 VI_2 | II_5^6 V | IV_2 VII_6 |

VI III_3^4 | VI_3^4 VI_5^6 | II I_6 | VII_5^6 VI | II_5^6 V | I ‖

13. g♯ $\frac{2}{2}$

I | II_2 ×VII_7 | III × VI_7 | II_3^4 V_7 | I_4^6 VII_3^4 |

III × VI_7 | II_3^4 V_3^4 | I_3^4 IV_3^4 | VII_7 VI_5^6 | II_6 V_7 | I ‖

14. Bb $\frac{3}{4}$

VI_5^6 | IV_7 II_6 VII_7 | III_7 I_6 II_7 | V III_7 VI | IV_7 VII_3^4 I_6 I_3^4 |

Figured basses.

From this point, accidentals referring to the altered second, sixth, and seventh degrees in the minor mode will not be indicated in figured bass exercises. They must of course be supplied by the student when the context demands.

Outer voices given, no chords indicated. The type of exercise hitherto given at this point (soprano voice, with chords indicated) is replaced by the following, for reasons indicated on page 177. The effort should be made to choose the chord which is most appropriate to the context; and this, frequently, will be found to vary according to the particular position used (p. 177).

Poco adagio

(2)

Andante

(3)

Adagio

(4)

Soprano voice, no chords indicated.

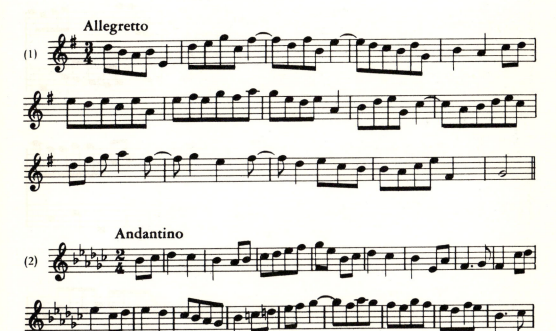

Allegro

(3)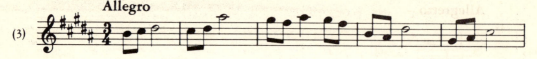

Adagio*

(4)

Vivace

(5)

* Accompaniment in eighth notes.

Allegretto

CHAPTER

SEVEN

Accessory Tones

1. EXTENDED USE OF ACCESSORY TONES

As already indicated in Chapter Five, the use of accessory tones, since very early times, has not been strictly confined to the simpler forms classified there. Composers have always allowed themselves whatever freedom they found consistent with clarity, and it is impossible to formulate binding principles in this respect. The following usages are all very familiar, and — though no guarantee can be given that any mode of procedure will invariably be of good effect — they may be employed without hesitation as a means to gaining more melodic and rhythmic resource and more freedom of movement.

Freer use of neighboring tones

1. The upper and the lower neighboring tones (p. 130), or vice versa, may be combined successively in a single ornament. (For illustration of this and the following freer uses, see the correspondingly numbered examples in Fig. 120.)

2. The melodic interval of a third may be bridged by the ornamental formula known as the "*Nota Cambiata*," in which a dissonant tone skips a third in the same direction in which it is moving, overleaping its goal, so to speak, by one degree — thus interpolating a neighbor-

ing tone between the passing tone (p. 130) and the tone of destination.

3. A neighboring tone may itself be preceded or followed, or both, by another neighboring tone.

4. A neighboring tone may follow a chordal tone without returning to it; or it may precede a chordal tone without being preceded by the same tone.

5. A consonant tone or a dissonant neighboring tone may be introduced between a suspension (p. 132) and its resolution.

Freer use of passing tones and anticipations

6. A single passing tone may occasionally be used to fill an interval greater than a third. In this case, however, it is generally — though not always — better that it be preceded rather than followed by a skip, and then proceed stepwise to its destination.

7. An anticipation (p. 131) may be "indirect" — that is, it may anticipate a tone in another voice of the following chord.

FIG. 120 *(1)*

VII₆   IV₆   V₇   * *   I⁶₄   VI   * *   VI   V₆   I

I₆   VI₆   I   V₆   VI   V   I   I   II₆   VI   I₆

IV   II   V₇   I   I   VI   II₆   II   V₇   I'

IV   I   VI   II   I   IV

The above are not all of the possible freer uses, and in general it may be said that the freedom with which accessory tones may be used will depend on the strength and definiteness of the harmonic support. If that support is firm enough and clear enough, any note or combination of notes may be introduced in an accessory sense, provided this is done for a clear melodic or linear purpose. As in so many other instances, the student should proceed cautiously in this respect, and try above all to gain sureness of instinct for the relationship between the *technical means which he is using*, and the *actual effect which he wishes to produce*. He should strive above all for clarity and precision, and for the utmost awareness, at this point, of every step which he takes. Only in this manner can he gain the real freedom of expression which his technical studies should foster.

Exercises

Soprano voice, with chords indicated.

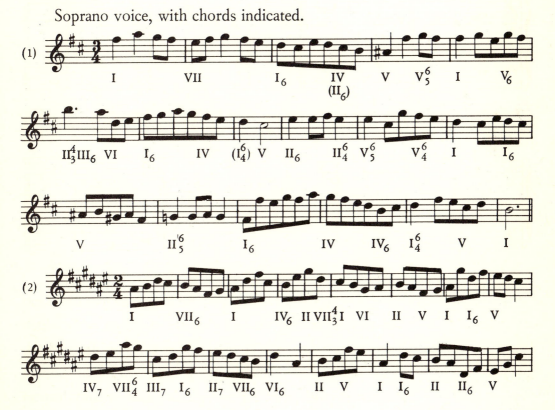

* Query: what constitutes the logical justification, in this specific instance, of the progression II_2–VI_2–II_5^6?

Outer voices given, no chords indicated.

Andante

(2)

Adagio

(3)

Andantino

(4)

Soprano voice, no chords indicated.

(1)

(2)

2. ACCESSORY TONES IN TWO OR MORE VOICES SIMULTANEOUSLY

Accessory tones may be used in two or more voices simultaneously. In strict counterpoint the rule is that, when only two voices are involved, such tones should always form consonant intervals — the interval of a fourth being classified with the dissonances and therefore prohibited; when three or more voices are involved, the accessory tones should form triads, six-chords, or six-four chords, care being taken to avoid consecutive octaves. Considerably more freedom may be allowed here; the question to be asked in each instance is whether the sounds produced in this manner do not contrast so violently with the sonorities established as the basis of the harmony as to throw the detail into undue relief.

Consecutive fifths are permissible if one of the fifths is formed by an accessory tone and a chordal tone, or by two different types of accessory tone — e.g., a passing tone and an anticipation. (See, for example, Fig. 121 (a); here the C in the first fifth is a suspension, while the E in the second fifth is an accented passing tone.)

FIG. 121

I   VI   (IV) (I₆) I   V   VI   II   V   I

* Accessory tone.

Great care must be taken, in the use of accessory tones, against an undue overloading of the texture. If the detail is too elaborate, the effect will be too heavy for the tempo desired and the emphasis to be produced. It is of paramount importance that the precise effect be clearly and vividly envisaged at every moment in the production of music. Compare, in this connection, pages 77–78.

3. PEDAL POINT

The device known as *"pedal point"* (or "organ point") may be considered here as not unrelated to the question just discussed — i.e., accessory tones in several voices at the same time. Actually, the pedal point is a means of prolonging a fundamental harmony while the process of elaboration goes on in other voices.

A "pedal point" is a tone which is held while the harmony moves in other voices, quite independently of it. Though most frequently found in the bass — hence the term, derived from the organ pedal — it may also be found in the other voices. The first and last chords of the "pedal" passage must be harmonies to which the "pedal" note belongs, but the others may be, and nearly always to some extent will be, foreign to it.

FIG. 122

I   II   III   IV   I   V   I   II   V₇   VI   III   II   V₇   I

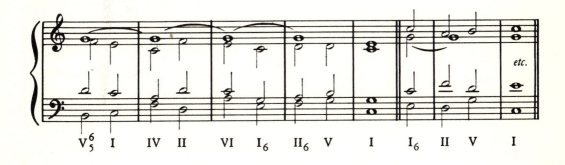

V⁶₅   I   IV   II   VI   I₆   II₆   V   I   I₆   II   V   I

etc.

Double and triple pedals, in which two or three notes
are held, are also possible — or even pedals consisting of
four or more held notes. (The latter are, however, obviously not practical in four voices.)

FIG. 123

etc.

The use of the pedal is unrestricted except by the demands of musical movement and proportion. Its effect is
to bind together the whole passage which it includes into
a single larger harmonic unit; it therefore occurs most
frequently (1) on the primary degrees of the key, especially v and i, and (2) at those points in a composition
where a single harmony is sustained for a period sufficiently long to demand a form of elaboration which will
bring the necessary variety and movement without at any
point compromising the harmonic effect.

4. HARMONIC ELABORATION

The student should now take note of certain musical
processes which, although their full implication stretches
beyond the limits of "harmony" proper, are nevertheless
inherent in the harmonic thinking and practice of composers, and which will be found helpful in understanding
many of the principles, and carrying out many of the exercises, to be found later in this book. These are the
processes of *harmonic elaboration*.

The prolongation of chords through elaboration   First of all, harmonies, in actual practice, do not necessarily take the form of *chords*. The latter may be broken (Fig. 124), and, in the form of broken chords,

FIG. 124 *(a)*   BACH, *Suite for Violoncello in E♭*

E♭ I

(b) MOZART, *Piano Sonata in D* (K. 576) *(c)*   WAGNER, *Das Rheingold*

D I   V   E♭ I

may be given characteristic rhythmic shape (Fig. 125).

            SCHUBERT,
FIG. 125 *(a)* Symphony No. 9 in C *(b)*   BEETHOVEN, *Sonata*, Op. 57

C I   f I

This does not exclude the use of accessory tones (Fig. 126).

FIG. 126 *(a)*

BEETHOVEN, *Sonata for Violoncello and Piano*, Op. 102, No.2 *(b)*   SCHUBERT, *Symphony No. 9 in C*

D I   C I

                                                          BRAHMS, *Violin Concerto*

(c)

D I

A harmony may be embodied in a scale (Fig. 127)

FIG. 127

(a)

BEETHOVEN, *Sonata for Violoncello and Piano,* Op. 102, No.2

(b)

BACH, *Chromatic Fantasy*

D V
dI
VII

(c)

SCHUMANN, *Piano Quintet,* Op. 44

E♭ V
I

or in a motif derived from the scale (Fig. 128).

FIG. 128 (a)

BACH, *Organ Fugue in D* (b)

BEETHOVEN, *Quartet,* Op. 95

D I
f I

(c)

WAGNER, *Die Walküre*

d I

It is impossible, here as elsewhere, to give an adequate classification of the various forms which a single harmony may take. *What should be kept in mind is that a "harmony" is, as it were, the extension of a single tone, the "root."* It follows, therefore, that any musical passage in which the harmonic sense of a single root is clearly felt — in which the sensation or effect is clearly unified in this respect — may be considered as the elaboration of a single harmony. Additional examples will help make this clearer.

FIG. 129   BEETHOVEN, *Quartet*, Op. 59, No. 1

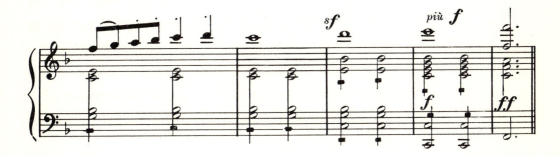

It would be false to regard the opening of this example as a I_4^6 chord, as may be clearly demonstrated if one compares the actual effect to that produced by the addition of an F from the very beginning, i.e.:

The harmony is incomplete until the F is sounded in measure 1 (at *):

thus, as it were, "closing the circuit" and completing the definition of the harmony. The passage is also an excellent illustration of the fact that a single consonant harmony may, through elaboration, be shaped in such a way as to produce an effect of suspense or tension analogous to that generally associated with the use of dissonance (pp. 14–15).

The following are still more elaborate:

FIG. 130

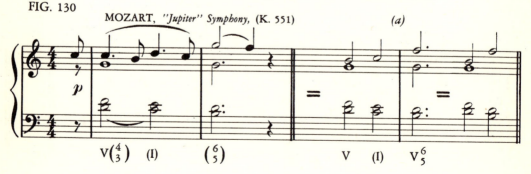

BEETHOVEN, *Symphony No. 3, "Eroica", Op. 55*

The examples in Figure 130 may be, of course, regarded as pedal points on the dominant; though it would perhaps be still more helpful to note the linear logic of the voice leading and to regard the chords at the points (a) as triple passing tones. More important than classification is the harmonic unity of each example. Both are instances of the elaboration, or prolongation, of the dominant harmony, and illustrations of the principle of *harmonic elaboration* or *prolongation* as such — a principle, and a process, which plays a major role in the technique of composition. This principle has already been mentioned in connection with the deceptive cadence (p. 86), the six-four chord (pp. 144–149), and the pedal point (pp. 199–200).

The following may now be considered:

FIG. 131 *(a)*   BEETHOVEN, *Quartet in F Minor*

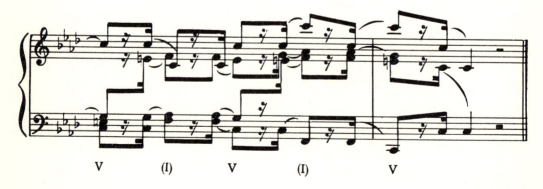

In Figure 131 (a) it is clear at point (x) that the harmonies v and I are derived from the dominant chord and its double neighboring tones which take shape as I_4^6, the latter being further elaborated by the addition of the root F, as

— just as, for instance, the figure

may be elaborated as

or

without destroying the essential unity of the tonic harmony.

In Figure 131 (b), the motif which has already been cited (Fig. 126 (c)) as an elaboration of the D major tonic triad is further elaborated by the harmonization of its separate tones. The D major triad, clearly embodied in the melodic line, dominates and unifies the whole passage; the harmonies set the various tones in greater relief and give them greater emphasis and weight, without destroying the sense of the passage. An excellent simple demonstration of the principle involved here is to be

FIG. 131 *(b)*

BRAHMS, *Violin Concerto* (Op. 77)

found in the closing measures of Richard Strauss's *Ein Heldenleben*, which "elaborate" and thus "prolong" the

R. STRAUSS, *Ein Heldenleben*

FIG. 132

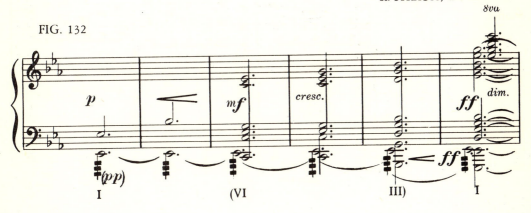

triad of E-flat, which in turn has been amply prepared by the dominant, in preceding measures.

In the following example, the elaboration lies in the

FIG. 133

BEETHOVEN, *Symphony No. 5,* Finale

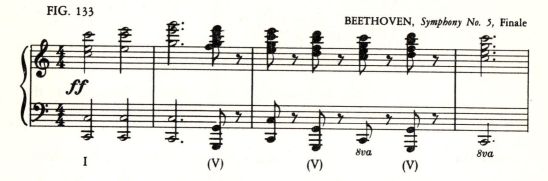

harmonization of tones which, considered from the standpoint of the C major triad, are passing or neighboring tones. (Actually, in the passage from which Figure 133 is quoted, the first essential change of harmony may be considered as occurring only at measure 14, in which the conclusive dominant harmony of the whole period is finally reached in the first of three successive repetitions.)

In accordance with the principle illustrated, such a passage as

may be elaborated, for example, thus:

The following is a more elaborate illustration of the same principle:

FIG. 134 BACH, *Prelude in F Sharp Minor,* Well Tempered Clavier, Book II

The deceptive cadence has already been discussed as a means of delaying the resolution of the dominant to the tonic; this means, in another sense, prolonging the dominant harmony. It is not necessary at this point to add further examples to those already cited (pp. 86, 161).

The prolongation of the dominant by the six-four chord has also been mentioned (p. 146), as has the elaboration of the latter chord in the cadenza of the classic concerto and in similar situations, e.g., measures 313–351 of Beethoven's *Sonata for Violoncello and Piano in F Major* (Op. 5, No. 1).

Because of its function as the upper fifth of the tonic, and the consequent fact that it is so often used as a "preparation" for the tonic harmony, the dominant harmony is peculiarly subject to prolongation — a prolongation which is, in fact, an extremely characteristic and essential technical feature of the music of the last three centuries. Psychologically, this means prolongation of the suspense with which the resolution to the tonic harmony is awaited, and it is, therefore, a very frequently employed means whereby important moments in the music — for example, contrasting ideas, or definitive returns to the tonic key — are introduced; in particular, its usefulness for dramatic purposes, e.g., in opera, is obvious. The pedal point, the deceptive cadence, and the six-four chord are perhaps the three most frequently used means in this prolongation, but composers have drawn on all the technical means at their disposal for this purpose. In his analysis of such instances in musical literature, the student will find it necessary, in most cases, to refer to the subjects still to be studied in the later chapters of this book — especially Chapters Eight, Ten, and Twelve.

Parallel chords and sequences

It will be clear from the above that harmonic elaboration, as described in these pages, is one of the principal means through which music is organized on a large scale. It is, for instance, at the very core of what is called the "symphonic" technique, as developed by Haydn, Mozart, and Beethoven; by its means, "harmonic rhythm" is organized on the largest possible scale, the "harmonic structure" thus obtained being clearly underlined by contrasts of other kinds: thematic contrasts, dynamic contrasts, contrasts of movement or of rhythmic detail, and contrasts of instrumentation or texture.

The concept of harmonic elaboration helps us also to understand the respective roles which are played by root progression and voice leading in the genesis of chords. In the elaboration of a single root harmony, or even in the transition from one root harmony to another, many chords will inevitably occur, as a result of elaboration, which have no real root sense whatever. In each of the following, for instance:

FIG. 135 *(a)*   BEETHOVEN, *Sonata,* Op. 10 No. 3

D V (I)   V   (III)   I

(b)   HAYDN, *Quartet,* Op. 76, No. 1

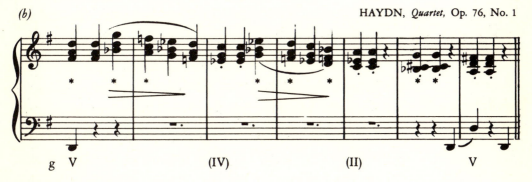

g V   (IV)   (II)   V

BEETHOVEN, *Concerto No. 4,* Op. 58

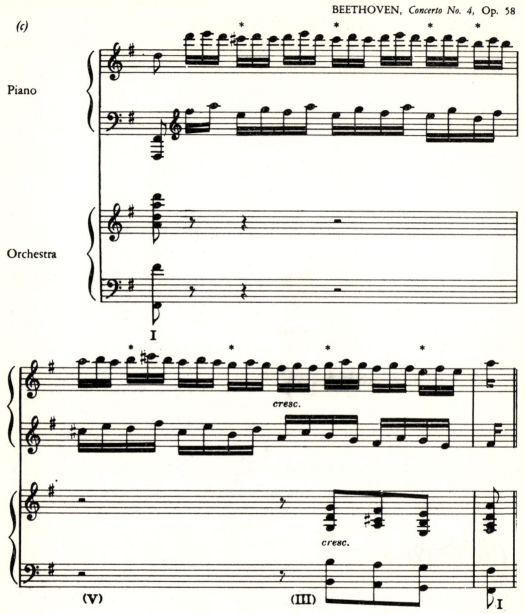

the chords indicated by (*) are clearly transitional in character; root relationships are felt only between the points indicated by Roman numerals, and even the

Roman numerals given in parentheses may be regarded as incidental to the larger elaboration.

The same is true on a much larger and more elaborate scale in such passages as:

Beethoven, *Symphony No. 5* (Op. 67), first movement, measures 196–229 (elaboration of IV_6–V);

Brahms, *Piano Quintet* (Op. 34), first movement, measures 81–85 (II_6, I_6–IV_6, I_4^6, V);

Beethoven, *Symphony No. 9* (Op. 125), first movement, measures 132–145 (I, VII_6–V_6, I_6–IV_6, V, I).

The parallel six-chords which form the basis of each of these passages are clearly transitional in character, and the essential root relationships are in each case the relationships between the chords of departure and the chords of destination, as indicated in the references.

A technique of transition similar to the foregoing, but more elaborate, is that of the *"sequence."* Instead of parallel chords, the sequence involves successive repetitions, on different degrees of the scale, of the same melodic and harmonic pattern, e.g.:

FIG. 136 *(a)*   BACH, *Prelude in C Sharp Minor*, Well-Tempered Clavier, Book I

V ———— VI_2 II_6 V_2 I_6

BEETHOVEN, *Quartet in C Sharp Minor* Op. 131

(b)

cresc.

IV₂   VII₆   III

E   VI   IV₄   VII   V₄   I   VI₄   II   VII₄   III
(BIV)   ₃   ₃   ₃   ₃

Though sequences move most frequently along successive degrees of the scale, Figure 135 (a) above may be taken as an example of a sequence of which the successive steps are each a third apart. Figure 135 (b) belongs to the same category; a single sequential repetition, however, is not generally classified as a sequence proper. The term "sequence" is generally applied to patterns of at least three steps.

The more complex the pattern, the less it will stand literal repetition without producing the effect of monotony. Very frequently, therefore, the need will be felt to vary the pattern on its third appearance (Fig. 137,

FIG. 137

BACH, *Fugue in C Minor*, Well-Tempered Clavier, Book I

C I   IV   VII   III

VI   II   V

measure 3), or, in the case of a prolonged sequence, the regularity of the pattern will be broken (Fig. 138).

FIG. 138

BACH, *Fugue in C Minor*, Well-Tempered Clavier, Book I

g   I   V   IV   V   I

C   VII   I

It should be noted that the term "sequence" applies only to regular repetitions of the same pattern, as illustrated above. Since the diatonic scale consists of semitones as well as whole tones, and furnishes the bass of major,

minor, diminished, and augmented triads, the intervals
will not necessarily exactly correspond in each successive
step. But such instances as the following are not sequential, since the harmonies do not correspond in a sequential manner.

FIG. 139 (a)

BEETHOVEN, *Quartet in E Flat*, Op. 127

MOZART, *Symphony in G Minor* (K.550)

The sequence is a technical device which is adaptable
to many varied uses, and further references to it will be
made in later chapters. It is essentially a means of transition from one well-established harmonic point to another,
and its aptness will depend to a large extent on the relationship between its first and final harmonies. When applied strictly to the diatonic scale, its actual technique
presents few problems; problems arise, however, when it
is applied in a modulatory, or tonally shifting, sense (see
pp. 313 ff.).

The sequence is also a device which, obviously, can be abused, since it can so easily become mechanical in effect, or a cliché, in the hands of an untalented or unskillful composer. Properly understood, however, it is a valuable means of transition, as it enables the composer to move from one point to another in an easy and relaxed fashion. By its means the transition from one harmony to another may be prolonged; and, like the elaboration of single harmonies, it has always played an important role in the organization of large-scale musical design. Primarily, the sequence should be understood in the sense of a transitional device, essentially linear in character, in spite of the fact that its details may be strictly in accordance with the principles of root progression.

Vertical and horizontal principles

It should be clear that the above pages, which deal with harmonic elaboration or prolongation, contain only the barest introduction to a practically inexhaustible subject. The material is introduced here, first, in order to open to the student a means of understanding some of the problems which will arise in connection with the later exercises in this book; secondly, to help him to grasp more clearly the real meaning of the principles of root relationship and root progression in terms of large musical design, and to gain a clear conception of the relationship between the "harmonic," or "*vertical*," principle of root progression on the one hand, and the "linear," "contrapuntal," or "*horizontal*" logic of voice leading on the other.

Exercises

Soprano voice, no chords indicated.

(1)

(2)

(3)

(4)

(5)

(6)

(7)

(8)

5. "FROZEN" ACCESSORY TONES

The use of dissonance in the music of the past hundred years has been, to a considerable extent, the result of the tendency of accessory tones to become "frozen," as it were, onto the harmonies with which they are associated. Repeated usage, that is, has made certain formulas so familiar that composers have, by a kind of condensation, added them in a vertical (or simultaneous) sense to the chords of departure or resolution.

Thus, the seventh chord, for instance, probably owes its origin to the "freezing" of a passing tone which habitually led from the root of one chord to the third of the following chord, according to the evolution illustrated below.

FIG. 140 (a)   (b)   (c)

IV I_4^6 V_7 I   IV I_4^6 II_5^6 I_4^6

In the course of the last hundred years, this process has become more and more frequent, and many chords which do not fall into easy classification are most simply defined in these terms.

Ninth, eleventh, and thirteenth chords

Such a chord, for instance, is the "ninth chord," which is generally classified as a basic chord type, but which presents certain definite peculiarities.

It will be noted, for instance, that the ninth can be resolved without changing the harmony, since the note of resolution is already present in the chord as its root.

FIG. 141

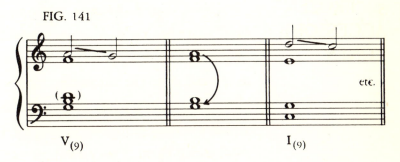

$V_{(9)}$ $I_{(9)}$

As a result of this fact, it is clear that while the seventh of the chord must in general be held until the resolution takes place, the ninth may be dropped, leaving only the seventh, without any serious loss of dissonant effect.

FIG. 142

V_9 $_7$ I II_9 $_7$ V II_7 II   V V_7 V   I

Inversions of the ninth chord are extremely varied in harmonic effect, even in the case of different positions of the same inversion. The following examples show in each case two different positions of the same inversion, which contain the same tones, but produce quite different harmonic effects; if they are played in alternation they seem to denote a genuine change in harmony.

FIG. 143

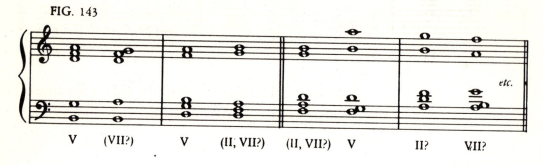

   V   (VII?)   V   (II, VII?)   (II, VII?) V   II?   VII?

For these reasons, it seems better to consider the ninth as an accessory note which habitual usage has "frozen" onto the chord. In most cases it will resolve one step downward in the usual manner; but other resolutions are also possible, as illustrated below.

FIG. 144

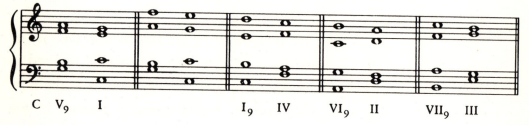

C V_9 I I_9 IV VI_9 II VII_9 III

$V^6_5{}^7$ I $V^6_{5\,4\,3}$ I_6 *but in* 4 *voices,* VII^6_5-I $V^{10}_{4\,2}$ I_6

The same observations are equally true in the case of the so-called chords of the "eleventh" and "thirteenth," as illustrated below.

FIG. 145

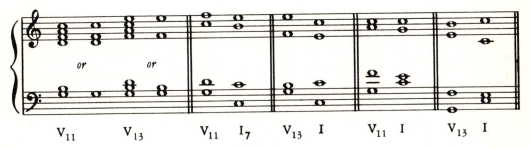

They are underlined by the fact that, in the case of the "eleventh" chord, the third is generally omitted in four-part or even five-part writing, since it is the note to which the eleventh would normally resolve. In the case of the "thirteenth" chord, the fifth is omitted as well as the eleventh, and in four-part writing, it is generally the ninth which is omitted, though the third is sometimes omitted if the ninth is present.

In the case of inversions of all of these chords, it is frequently impossible to classify a given instance as belonging to one degree or another. In the case, for instance, of ♭𝄞 , either C, as in ♭𝄞 , or B, as in

, could be considered the root, though both its structure and its most obvious resolution suggest that it is simplest to consider it as a six-four chord with added seventh.

In the overwhelming majority of cases, these chords are used on the dominant degree, but use on other degrees is also possible.

"Substitute functions"

Of a somewhat similar nature are what may be termed *"substitute functions"*; the term applies to cases in which a chord normally identified with one degree is used where the clear harmonic effect is that of another. The simplest of such cases is the fairly common substitution of a six-chord for the triad (whose root is two degrees higher than that of the six-chord in question) which would result if the sixth of the six-chord were lowered one step, thus becoming the fifth of the triad. Thus, in certain cases, III$_6$, for example, may be regarded as the equivalent of v, and the following illustration

FIG. 146

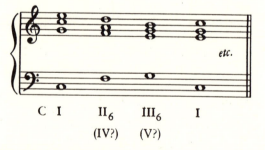

C I   II$_6$ III$_6$ I
           (IV?)   (V?)

seems obviously closer in effect to the cadence I–IV–V–I than to the root succession I–II–III–I.

In such cases it is, of course, normal to double the bass, not the root, of the six-chord in question.

The six-five chord is likewise frequently used in the manner of a triad with a "frozen" sixth, in which case it is the sixth which must be regarded as the added tone and which generally moves upward, the remainder of the chord being treated as an ordinary triad. The same process may also be applied to other positions of the seventh chord; this procedure is in general use, though it has not become a formula to the extent that the added sixth has. Examples:

FIG. 147

VI II⁶₅ I   I₆ III⁶₅ II₆ VII₆ I   IV VI₂ V₇   I

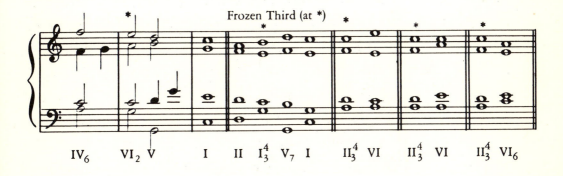

IV₆   VI₂ V   I   II   I⁴₃ V₇ I   II⁴₃ VI   II⁴₃ VI   II⁴₃ VI₆

V II⁴₃ I   II⁴₃ IV⁶₄ I   I₆ II⁴₃ I⁶₄ II₆ V I   I₆ IV⁶₅ I⁶₄ II₆

In all these cases, the "pull" of the linear impulse gives the added ("frozen") dissonance its motivation and makes its sense clear.

This concept leads us to further, hitherto unused forms, e.g.:

FIG. 148
Frozen Seventh (at *)

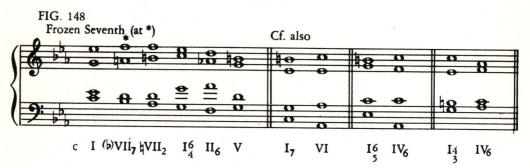

Cf. also

Such usages as those just described are general in application, and hence can easily be classified. On the other hand, the student will in the course of his analytical study come across some instances in which a harmonic progression of clearly defined sense is *contracted*, through the omission of a chord which belongs literally to the progression in question, but which is, as it were, taken for granted. To such a category belong, for instance, the occasional cases in which a cadential I_4^6 chord moves directly to the tonic, without the intervention of the dominant chord. Such instances as Beethoven, *Symphony No. 9* (Op. 125), first movement, measures 34–35, or R. Strauss, *Domestic Symphony* (Op. 53), measures 8–9 after No. 77 (p. 61 of the orchestral score), belong to the category of refinements — of individual cases, that is, into which other factors than the apparent progression I_4^6–I come into consideration. In both of the above the strong accentuation of the dominant tone in the bass, on the beat before the resolution to the tonic, has the force of the dominant harmony; and other elements — the analysis of which would be too long to include here — contribute to the satisfying effect. (Cf. also Verdi, *Falstaff*, Act III, Part 2, from two measures before No. 55 through Falstaff's words "*Tutto in mondo è burla*" at the beginning of the final fugue.)

While the frozen accessory tones classified above are the most common, many others are possible, of course. The student thus may — and should — experiment freely, bearing in mind always the real demands of a given situation and the appropriateness of the effect in question, and also the fact that with the means thus far at his disposal no very unusual effects are possible.

Exercises

Figured basses.

Soprano voice, with chords indicated.

Outer voices given, no chords indicated.

Andante

Allegro

(2)

(V)

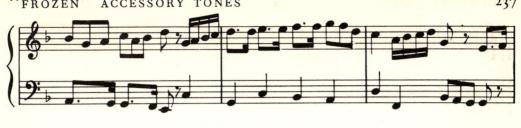

Presto

(3)

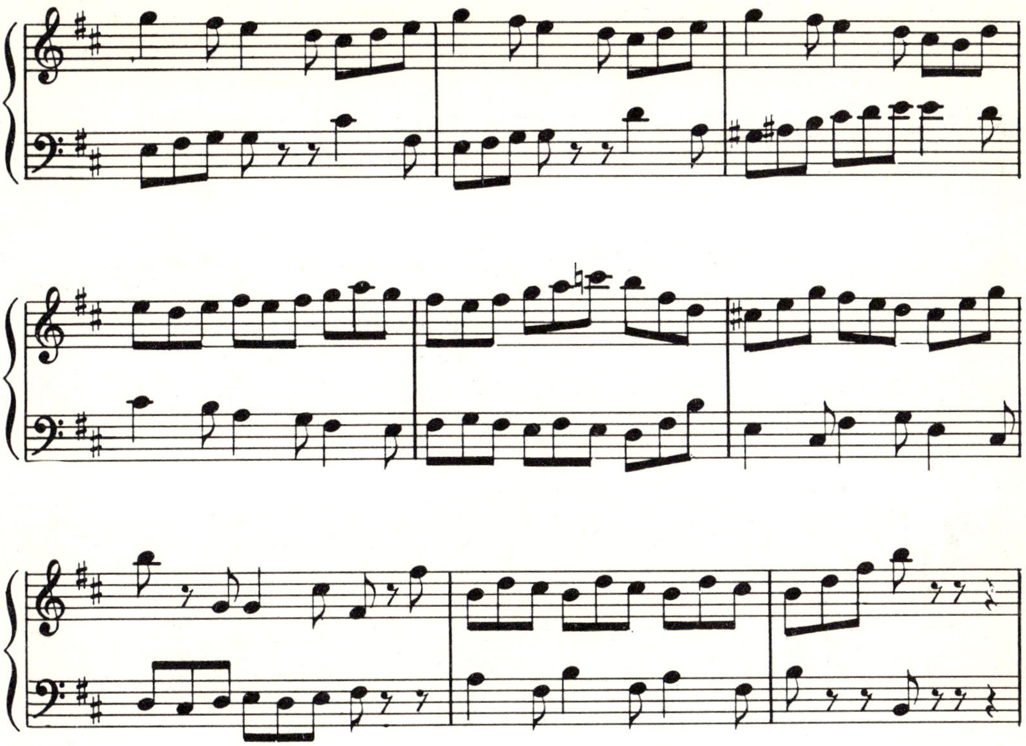

Soprano voice, no chords indicated.

(1)

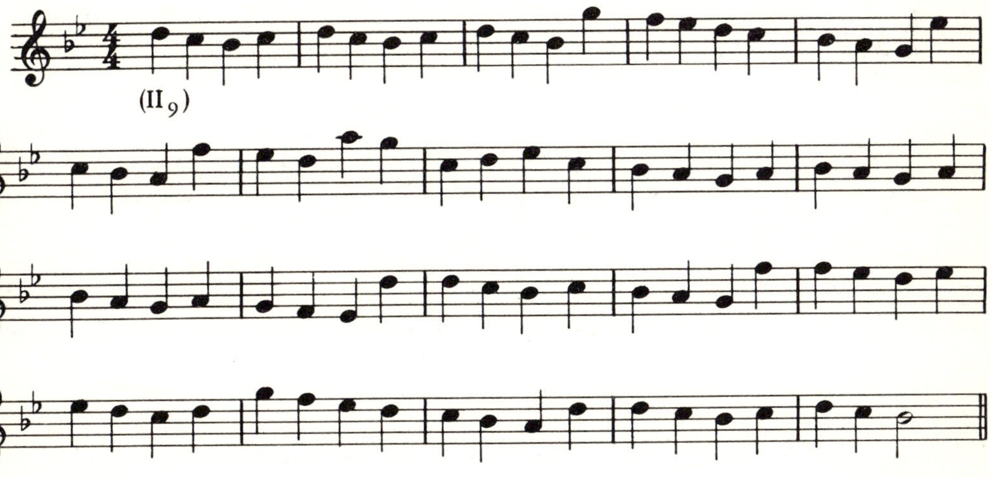

(2)

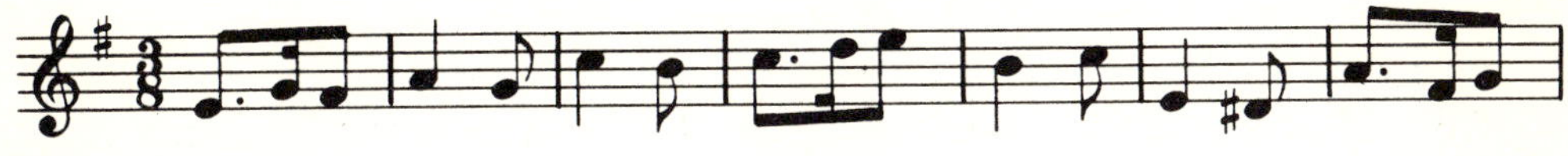

(3)

(4)

(5)

(8)

CHAPTER

EIGHT

Tonicization

Harmonies other than the tonic are often given greater vividness or emphasis by means of a process which may be called "*tonicization*" (see p. xvii). In its simplest form this process consists in giving the harmony in question the temporary aspect of a tonic, thus strengthening it in its individual character and, so to speak, drawing it momentarily away from its place in the prevailing key, into a quasi-key of its own.

Though the process is not unlike modulation, it differs clearly from the latter in scope and function. "Modulation" denotes a definitive change of key — a decisive movement to a fresh tonal region — and, from the standpoint of composition, has to do with the larger features rather than the details of a musical work. What we call tonicization, however, is essentially a matter of detail.

1. SECONDARY DOMINANT, LEADING–TONE, AND OTHER HARMONIES

While modulation proper involves definite harmonic and rhythmic goals, and most often requires a progression of several chords, tonicization can be, and most often is, accomplished by a single "secondary" chord, most often a secondary dominant or leading-tone chord, which derives its tonicizing function from alteration.

If, for example, VI in the key of C is tonicized in this manner, the preceding chord will be some form of either III♯ or ♯V, III♯ being the secondary dominant, and ♯V the secondary leading-tone chord, of VI.

FIG. 149

I	V of VI	VI		I	VII₆ of VI	VI
	= III♯				= ♯V₆	

The secondary dominant chord may take the form of V, V₆, V₇, V₅⁶, V₃⁴, V₂, V₉, or derivatives of the latter; the secondary leading-tone chord may take that of VII₆, VII₇, VII₅⁶, VII₃⁴, or VII₂, with VII₇ and its inversions appearing most often, though not always, in the form of the diminished seventh chord (p. 164), which may now be resolved freely to major as well as to minor triads (cf. Chapter Ten).

In the following example (Fig. 150), the secondary dominant and leading-tone chords are written in black notes. The figures above the black notes indicate the types of relationship to the chords that follow; the figures underneath indicate, as usual, the relationships of all chords to the tonic, and, therefore, the sense of the progression as a whole.

FIG. 150

Less frequently, tonicization may be effected on the basis of relationships other than those of the dominant and leading tone, e.g.:

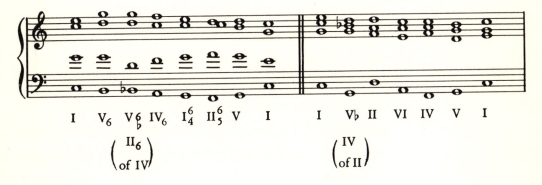

FIG. 151 *(a)*   *(b)*

A secondary dominant or leading-tone chord may also be resolved in the manner of a deceptive cadence:

FIG. 152

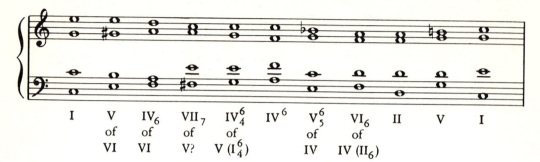

I	V	IV₆	VII₇	IV⁶₄	IV⁶	V⁶₅	VI₆	II	V	I
	of	of	of	of		of	of			
	VI	VI	V?	V (I⁶₄)		IV	IV (II₆)			

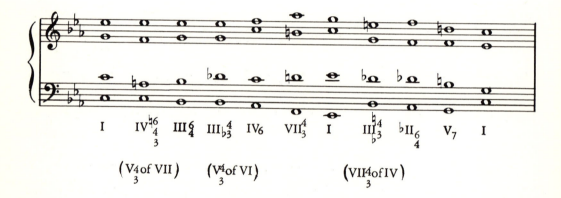

I	IV⁴⁶₄₃	III⁶₄	III♭⁴₃	IV₆	VII⁴₃	I	III♭³⁴₃	♭II₆₄	V₇	I

(V⁴₃ of VII)   (V⁴₃ of VI)   (VII⁴₃ of IV)

or may be treated in the manner of a half cadence:

FIG. 153 *(a)*

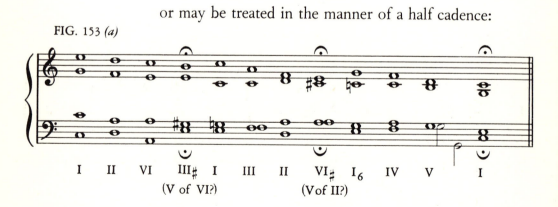

I	II	VI	III♯	I	III	II	VI♯	I₆	IV	V	I
			(V of VI?)				(V of II?)				

(b)

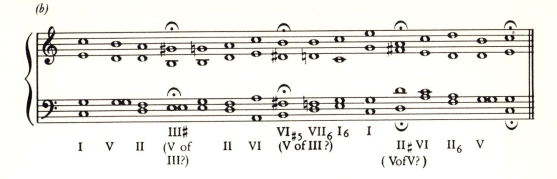

In these latter cases the tonicization does not really take shape, since the tonicized chord does not actually appear. In Figure 152, the tonicized chords are by-passed by the "deceptive" resolution. In Figure 152 (a) the individual alterations are perhaps motivated by the leading of the voices in which they occur, rather than by the root relationships involved. Figure 152 (b) presents instances in which the deceptive resolutions are more pronounced in the strictly harmonic sense; where the alterations, in other words, are less clearly motivated by the voice leading, and more by the refinements of the root progression. The ear perceives clearly that the theoretically "tonicized" chords are by-passed, and that the progression is, as it were, carried beyond them by the substitute chords which actually occur. It will be noted in this connection that the deceptive resolution of a secondary dominant does not necessarily imply a prolongation of the latter; since the dominant is "secondary" — that is, subordinate to a harmony other than the tonic — it is less forceful in its harmonic effect than the primary dominant.

In Figure 153 (a) the tonicized harmonies precede the

secondary dominants, and are, so to speak, tonicized in retrospect, while in Figure 153 (b) they have become independent harmonic goals. The term "tonicization," however, is applicable to this as to the other cases, and it should be understood as referring to a harmonic *process*, or *line of thought* — one which first of all establishes certain secondary relationships within the orbit of the key, including especially the secondary dominant harmonies. But, as a further development of the same process, these secondary relationships sometimes achieve independent value, and can be used — as above illustrated (Figs. 152, 153) — in contexts other than those which originally gave rise to them.

2. ALTERED ACCESSORY TONES

To the same line of thought, though on a minute scale, belong certain very commonly used alterations of accessory tones.

It is, for instance, the rule rather than the exception to treat a lower neighboring tone or appoggiatura as a kind of "secondary leading tone" by raising it chromatically, in order to let it move a semitone instead of a larger interval, e.g.:

FIG. 154

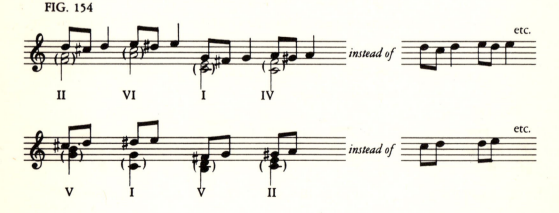

VII   III   III   II

However, this procedure is exceptional in the case of the appoggiatura which resolves to the raised seventh degree (the leading tone) in the minor mode, since if the raised sixth is so altered, the ear is likely to confuse the resulting tone with the unaltered seventh. The same is true, though to a lesser degree, in the major mode:

FIG. 155

more often than

On the other hand, the alteration downward of an upper neighboring tone is more problematical, since it tends in many cases to confuse and thus to weaken the sense of the harmony in question. The following examples (Fig. 156), to be read as in C major, should help to make this clear.

FIG. 156

C   I (or f V?)   II (or B♭ III?)   IV   VI (or f III?)

C VI II III

C IV VII

and tonicize II and IV respectively, and are therefore good.

For the sense of the following, all of which are possible and essentially unproblematical, see Chapter Ten.

FIG. 157

C I V V VII

In the various forms of the melodic ornament or elaboration known as the "*turn*," both the lower semitone and the upper tone or semitone are used, e.g.:

· FIG. 158

BEETHOVEN, *Concerto in G*, Op. 58

I II V I VI etc.

Chromatic passing tones may now be used:

FIG. 159   Cf. CHOPIN, *Étude*, Op. 10, No. 2

They are easily abused, however, and the student should use them sparingly in order to gain the greatest possible awareness of their real effect. The danger is that they offer a too easy method of sustaining a flow of movement at places where a diatonic pattern would be stronger, e.g.:

FIG. 160

will usually be found inferior to:

I₆   IV   V   **V₇**   I

There are, however, no dependable rules which can be formulated in regard to such matters, and the student must cultivate his own judgment and rely on it.

Altered accessory tones, like unaltered ones, can be used in two or three voices at the same time:

FIG. 161

C   I   I₆   V   V₂   I₆

MOZART, *Concerto*, K 450   BACH, *Brandenburg Concerto No. 1*

3. TONICIZATION AND HARMONIC ELABORATION

The materials studied in this chapter offer, of course, important new resources for harmonic elaboration (pp. 202 ff.). It will be readily seen that tonicization is in itself a form of elaboration, or prolongation; in Figure 150, for instance, the harmonies of the basic progression (expressed in whole notes) are prolonged, respectively, by their secondary dominant and leading-tone chords. They are thrown into greater relief, thus not only giving greater length, but also enlarging what may be called the *harmonic span* of the progression. By giving each step in the progression the effect of a temporary tonic, the tonicization underlines the contrasts between the various steps; for it weakens their functional dependence on each other, making of each a kind of tonal subcenter, with its secondary dominant or leading-tone chord, to which other dependent harmonies could be added in further elaboration. The sense of the progression, however, would always remain the same, provided that the primary relationships of tonic, dominant, and subdominant were present in adequate proportions and were not strongly overbalanced by a too preponderant elaboration of the secondary harmonies.

Actually, any harmony that is held or prolonged will tend to assume the character of a tonic, unless the prolongation is such as to strongly emphasize relationships which are inconsistent with that character. Even if such relationships *are* emphasized, the tendency will be for the chord that is prolonged to assume the character of a dominant or a subdominant (rather than that of one of the secondary chords), as the elaboration or the context emphasizes the relationship of the harmony in question with its upper or its lower fifth.

The reason for this is clear. A single consonant chord, in the absence of any context, will always be felt as a tonic chord; a relationship of two chords whose roots are a fifth apart will tend to have the effect of v–i (or i–v) unless the chord of the upper fifth is a minor triad, in which case the relationship will more likely be interpreted by the ear as i–iv, or — if the chord of the lower fifth is major — ii–v, the tritone formed by the root of the one chord, and the third of the other, being decisive in this case.

The ear will always interpret relationships between tones in their simplest sense, and will modify its impressions only when it has become fully aware of a larger context. This "becoming aware of a larger context" is the main problem which the listener faces, in regard to music which is unfamiliar to him; and, on the other hand, the main technical problem of composition is that of establishing the larger context on clear and solid lines.

The following examples will illustrate some of the functions of tonicization in connection with harmonic elaboration:

1. Elaboration through tonicization of the harmony in question:

FIG. 162

BEETHOVEN, *Sonata*, Op. 57

I

V
(C I   (VII $\frac{4}{3}$)   I)

BRAHMS, *Symphony No. 3* (Op. 90)

I   V   IV   II   V
         F I (IV$_6$) I(IV$_6$ V)   I   (VI)

2. Incidental tonicization in the course of a larger elaboration:

FIG. 163

SCHUBERT, *Sonata*, A Major

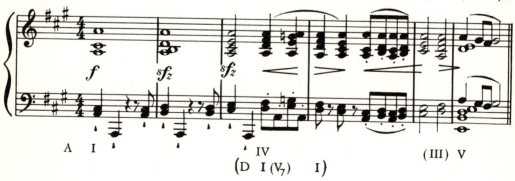

A I   IV   (III) V
      (D I (V$_7$)   I)

BEETHOVEN, *Sonata* ("Hammerklavier") Op. 106

3. Tonicization of the successive steps of a sequence (see also Figs. 132, 133):

FIG. 164   BEETHOVEN, *Symphony No. 3* ("Eroica") Op. 55

BEETHOVEN, *Symphony No. 5*

4. Tonicization in a progression of secondary dominants, transitional in character (Fig. 165). Compare pages 212–213.

In summary: any harmony may be tonicized, provided (1) the relief into which the tonicization throws the harmony in question is justified by the rhythmic or expressive context, or, in other words, that the tonicization is genuinely motivated, and (2) that the process of tonicization does not overload the general harmonic effect in such a way as to destroy the tonal balance or interfere with the clarity of the basic progression.

As in so many other connections, it is impossible to lay down fixed rules for the guidance of the student. His best course is to use this technique rather sparingly and with his attention first of all on the main task of achieving a satisfactory general harmonic effect. It is useless, in other words, for him to master the mechanics unless he is also gaining a sense for the principle which lies behind it, and the process of *"musical thought,"* meaning thought and expression *in* music (that is, in tones and rhythms), and not merely ideas *about* music.

FIG. 165

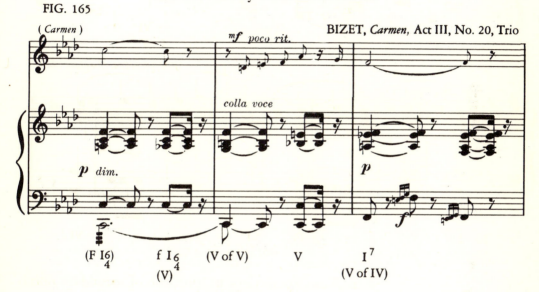

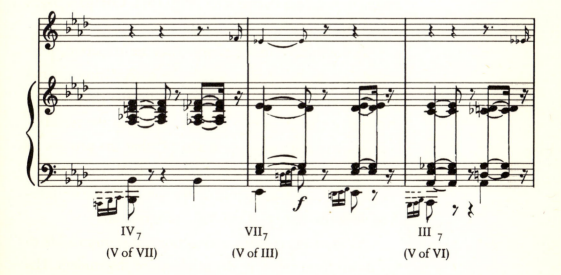

VI $_7$

(V of II)   II$_7$ V

Exercises

Figures only.

1. B♭ I$^2_5$–IV$_6$–I$^6_4$–IV–VII$_{♭7}$–I

2. e I–VII$_7$–I$^{8-7}_♯$–IV–$^♯$IV$^7_♯$–V$_7$–I

3. D I–$^♯_♯$I$_{♮7}$–II$_{8-7}$–I$^6_♯$–III–II$_6$–II–I$^6_4$–V$_7$–I

4. f I–VI–♮III$_{♭7}$–IV–♮IV$^7_♮$–V$_♮$–IV$^6_♮$–♮VII$_7$–I

5. E I–III$_♯$–IV–II–V$_7$–$^♯$I$^4_{♮3}$–II$^6_♯$–III$^6_5$–VI–IV–II–I$^6_4$–V–I

6. c I–IV$^6_5$–♭VII$_7$–III$_{♭7}$–VI–$^♯$IV$^6_5$–I$^6_4$–V$^7_♮$–I

7. B I–II$^{♯4}_2$–V$_6$–II$^{♮6}_4$–※VII$_7$–VI–II$^6_5$–I$^6_4$–V–I

8. d I–III$^4_{♭3}$–IV$_6$–VII$_{♯5}$–III–I$^{♯6}_4$–IV–VII$^{♯4}_3$–I$_6$–

   II$^7_{♮5}$–V$_♯$–I$^7_♯$–IV–I$^6_4$–V–I

9. A♭ I–I$_{♭7}$–IV$^6_4$–VII$^7_{♮5}$–III–♮I$^6_5$–II$_6$–III$^6_5$–IV$_6$–V$^6_5$–I

10. c♯ I–II$^{♯5}_※$–V–III$_{♮7}$–VI–II$^6_5$–III$_6$–IV$^6_5$–$^♯$VII$_7$–I–VI$_{♮7}$–

    ♮II–V–I

11. D I–III$^{\sharp 6}_{4}{}_{3}$–VI–I$^{4}_{\natural 3}$–IV–I$^{\sharp 6}_{\natural 5}$–II$_6$–$\sharp$V$_7$–VI–IV–V–I

12. g I–III$_{\sharp 5}$–VI–IV$^6_5$–$\natural$VII–$\sharp$VII$^6_5$–III$_{\sharp 5}$–IV$_6$–I$^6_4$–V–I

13. E♭ I–III$^7_{♭5}$–IV–♭IV$_7$–III$^6_\natural$–VI–II$^6_5$–I$^6_4$–V–I

14. f♯ I–I$^7_\sharp$–IV$^6_4$–$\sharp$VII$_7$–I$^{\sharp 4}_2$–IV$_6$–V$^7_{\natural 5}$–VI–II$^{\sharp 5}_\sharp$–$\natural$VII–III$_{\natural 7}$– VI–II$^6_5$–V–I

Figured basses.

Soprano voice, with chords indicated.

Soprano voice, no chords indicated.

(2)

(3)

(4)

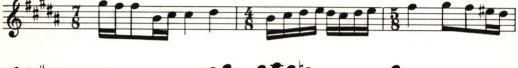

(7)

(8)

CHAPTER

NINE

Modulation (I) Using Only the Resources of the Unaltered Diatonic Scale

1.

THE NATURE OF MODULATION

As already indicated, modulation denotes a genuine change of key, and for this reason, in most cases, requires a more or less prolonged preparation, rather than a single relationship as in the case of a tonicized harmony. It should be stressed from the outset that a real modulation is a compositional as well as a purely harmonic process — that is, (1) a really convincing modulation must be carried by the rhythm and the melodic line as well as by the harmonies, and (2) its goal will be in the largest sense rhythmically as well as harmonically important. A modulation will coincide either with the final harmony of a phrase, sentence, or other rhythmic group, or with the initial harmonies of a contrasting rhythmic group. Finally, a modulation must eventually be conceived as a real transition. It is effective only if the musical context provides it with a point of departure, and a genuine musical goal, in what one may term an actual musical landscape.

A modulation must effect an association of ideas. Abstract exercises in modulation are therefore technically useful but aurally unconvincing, except as regards the smoothness of the progressions involved. Whether a given progression of chords constitutes a convincing modulation can be judged only in definite musical contexts in which more is involved than a mere change of harmony. Quite frequently it will be found in practice that a given modulation is not a matter of *chords* at all, and cannot be understood in any real sense by reducing it to a mere chordal progression. Thematic, structural, and even dynamic and instrumental (and perhaps, above all, *rhythmic*) factors — factors which have to do with the musical ideas and the composition — are always involved to some extent, and frequently bear the whole burden of the effect.

Such considerations come, of course, under the heading of composition rather than that of harmonic technique, and in any case they do not preclude the necessity of thorough mastery of the techniques of modulation by means of chords.

The problem is that of effecting a shift in tonal association, and may be envisaged as consisting of three essential points: (1) the point of departure in the original key; (2) a pivotal point, generally consisting of one or more "pivotal" harmonies which are common to both keys; and (3) the point of decisive contact with the new key, which must then be clearly established by means of a cadence or its equivalent. The modulation will not be really complete until a rhythmic as well as a harmonic goal has been reached, and will not be convincing unless the melodic as well as the harmonic design is convincing in terms of the key of destination.

**2.
MODULATION
THROUGH
PIVOTAL
CHORDS**

Modulation to the keys represented by the consonant triads within the original key (i.e., II, III, IV, V, VI in the major mode; III, IV, V, VI, VII in the pure minor mode) may be readily effected through the use of pivotal chords — i.e., chords which are common to both keys. Thus, in modulation from any key in the major mode to its dominant, I, III, V, or VI may be taken as pivotal harmonies, since the same chords are, respectively, IV, VI, I, and II, in the key of destination.

Similarly, in this case, II, IV, and VII, as well as the seventh chord of V, will not be available for this purpose since they all contain the fourth degree of the scale (e.g., in C major, F), which conflicts with the seventh degree of the new key (e.g., in the dominant of C major, F#).

The student should first investigate, according to the above pattern, all possible pivotal chords in each of the relationships listed above, i.e., in the major mode, I–II, I–III, I–IV, I–V, and I–VI (in C major, C–d, C–e, C–F, C–G, and C–a); in the minor mode, I–III, I–IV, I–V, I–VI, and I–VII (in c minor, c–Eb, c–f, c–g, c–Ab, c–Bb). E.g., modulation from C major to G major (I–V):

I in C is IV in G;
III " " " VI " ";
V " " " I " ";
VI " " " II " ";

or, modulating from c minor to Ab major (I–VI):

I in c is III in Ab;
III " " " V " ";
IV " " " VI " ";
VI " " " I " ".

The actual modulation can easily be effected by moving directly from the pivotal chord toward the cadence of the new key, e.g.:

FIG. 166

C I
G IV   V   I

or in more elaborate form, for example:

FIG. 167

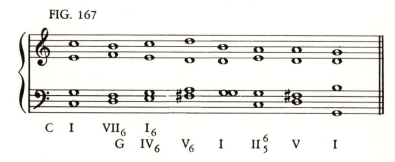

C I   VII$_6$ I$_6$
    G   IV$_6$ V$_6$ I   II$_5^6$ V   I

In the latter example, note the influence of the line of the soprano voice, leading down from the fifth to the first degree of the scale at the end, and the progression of the bass, leading steadily up to the tonic of G at the beginning, on the decisive effect of the modulation. Compare with the less decisive effect of the following which uses the same harmonies:

FIG. 168

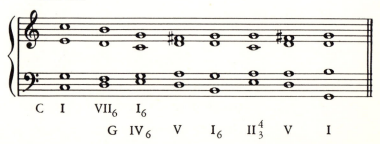

C I   VII$_6$ I$_6$
    G   IV$_6$ V   I$_6$ II$_3^4$ V   I

The principle involved here lies in conceiving both of the outer voices in terms of the key of destination — in this case, of course, G — from the outset of the modulation, including the point of departure in the first key. In the minor mode, e.g.:

FIG. 169

The prolongation at VI, above, is necessary since, until the subdominant harmony of A♭ is present, all of the associations are still those of c minor, with no D♭ present to contradict this.

If the key of destination is in the minor mode, the sixth and seventh degrees of this key should be treated from the outset of the modulation in the manner characteristic of the mode, e.g.:

FIG. 170 *(a)*   *(b)*

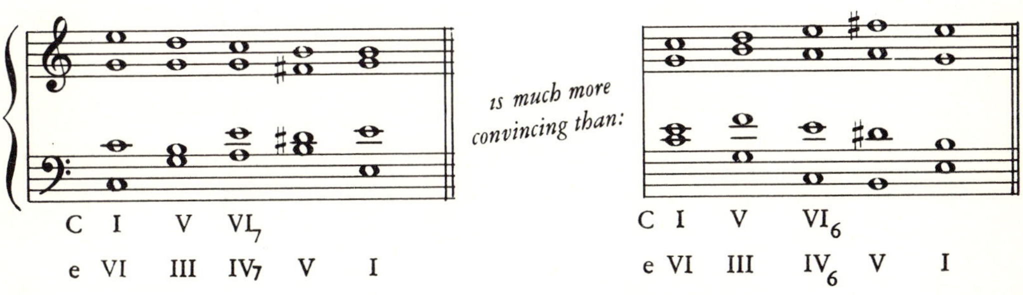

is much more convincing than:

The value of such observations is that of sharpening one's awareness of musical effect, however, and not of developing set modes of procedure. *It must be emphasized that the appropriateness of a line or a chord is the result always of a given context, and not of an abstract principle.* The problem for the student is to develop as ready a resourcefulness as he can; and to this end he should systematically explore all the possibilities, and develop his powers of observation to the utmost.

Exercises

Figures only.

1. Ab: I | V_6 | | (v)
   Eb: | I_6 II | I_4^6 V | I

2. b: I | V_6 | | (v)
   f#: | I_6 II_6 | I_4^6 V | I

3. F: I VI | III_6 | | (III)
   a: | I_6 IV_6 | I_4^6 V | I

4. c#: I III_6 | VI | | (VI)
   A: | I IV | V V_7 | I

5. D: I IV | II | | (II)
   e: | I IV_6 | I_6 V_7 | I

6. f: I | III_6 | | (III)
   Ab: | I_6 VI | II_5^6 V | I

7. E: I | VI | | (VI)
   c#: | I VI | II_5^6 V | I

8. g: I | VII_6 | | (VII)
   F: | I_6 IV_6 | I_4^6 V_7 | I

9. Db: I | IV_6 | | (IV)
   Gb: | I_6 IV_6 | I_4^6 V_7 | I

10. e: I | IV | | (IV)
    a: | I II_5^6 | I_4^6 V | I

11. B: I | | | (v)
    F#: IV VII_6 | I_6 IV_6 | II_5^6 V_7 | I

12. d: I | | (v)
    a: IV | II_3^4 I_4^6 | IV V_7 | I

13. Eb: I | | (VI)
    c: III | II_5^6 IV_6 | I_6 V_7 | I

14. f#: I | | (III)
    A: VI | III IV | I_4^6 V_7 | I

15. G: I | | (II)
    a: VII | IV_6 I_4^6 | II_5^6 V_7 | I

16. bb: I | | (VI)
    Gb: III VII_6 | I II_6 | II_3^4 V_7 | I

17. A: I | | (III)
    c#: VI | IV I_6 | II_7 V_7 | I

18. c: I | | (VII)
    Bb: II VII_5^6 | I_6 II_6 | I_4^6 V | I

19. F#: I | | (IV)
    B: V VI | IV I_6 | II_7 V_7 | I

20. a: I | | (IV)
    d: V VI_6 | $III_\sharp$ VI | II_5^6 V_7 | I

21. C: I_6 V_3^4 | VI_6 | | (v)
    G: | II_6 VII_5^6 | I_6 V_7 | I

22. eb: I | VI III | | (v)
    bb: | VI | II_5^6 V_7 | I

23. Bb: I_6 | IV | | (II)
    c: | III II_6 | I_4^6 V_7 | I

24. g#: I II_5^6 | III_6 | | (VII)
    F#: | IV_6 I_4^6 | II_5^6 V | I

25. E: I_6 IV | VI | | (III)
    g#: | IV ※VII_7 | I II_6 | I_4^6 V | I

26. f: I II_6 | III_6 | | (VI)
    Db: | V_6 I | II_5^6 V_7 | I

27. Ab: I₆ III₄⁶ | VI II | | | (IV)
Db: | | VI | II₅⁶ V₇ | I

28. b: I II₅⁶ | III₆ IV₆ | | | (IV)
e: | VII₆ I₆ | II₅⁶ V₇ | I

29. D: I | VII₃⁴ | | | (VI)
b: | II₃⁴ V♯ | I VI | II₅⁶ III♯⁶ | I

30. g: I III₇ | | (VII)
F: IV₇ | II₃⁴ V₇ | I

31. Eb: I | IV₇ | | (II)
f: | III₇ IV | I₄⁶ V | I

32. f♯: I II₅⁶ | | | (III)
A: VII₅⁶ | I₆ II₆ | I₄⁶ V | I

33. G: I I₂ | VI | | (III)
b: | IV II₃⁴ | I₄⁶ V | I

34. d: I IV₇ | | | (IV)
g: I₇ | II₅⁶ V | I

35. F♯: I ※I♮₇ | | | (II)
g♯: ※VII₇ | I VI | II₅⁶ V₇ | I

36. c: I ♮III♭₇ | IV | | (VI)
Ab: | VI II₅⁶ | I₄⁶ V₇ | I

37. Bb: I II₅⁶ | V | | (III)
d: | III VI₇ | II₅⁶ V₇ | I

38. eb: I VI | | | (V)
bb: ♭II | V₆ I₆ | II₅⁶ V | I

39. C: I | IV₆ | | | (III)
e: | ♮III₆ V | I₆ IV₆ | II₇ V₇ | I

40. c♯: I ♯VI♮₅⁶ | VII₆ | | (III)
E: | V₆ I | IV V₇ | I

Make each of the following modulations in four different ways, using each time a different pivotal harmony. Effect the modulations with as few chords as possible.

1. D–b   3. Bb–Eb   5. E–g♯   7. Ab–Eb   9. A–b
2. f–Ab   4. c♯–g♯   6. d–Bb   8. b–e   10. g–F

Figured basses.

Repeat exercises 1–10 (p. 273), using more chords
(not more than eight in each case) in order to strengthen

the modulation in each case through the movement of the outer voices.

3. HARMONI-ZATION OF CHORALES

The resources now at hand are quite sufficient to allow the student to undertake exercises in the harmonization of chorales. Such studies are valuable in giving a sharper sense of basic harmonic contrasts and relationships, as well as experience in planning fairly extended harmonic progressions toward clear harmonic goals. Furthermore, the chorales of Bach provide incomparable models with which the student can always compare his work, and from which he can always learn through study. Such study is highly to be recommended and can be extremely helpful if two important considerations are always kept in mind, namely:

First, leaving aside the fact that the student is dealing with the mature work of one of the greatest masters who ever lived (a fact of which the student will become more and more aware in proportion to the development of his musical insight), he should recognize that his aims are, and must necessarily be, quite different from those of Bach. The latter's aims were, in the most precise sense, creative; that is to say, he was concerned entirely with musical expression and was unrestricted in his choice of materials. The student is, at this point, pursuing strictly technical aims, with definitely restricted materials, and he will not get the full benefit from such exercises unless he subordinates other possible aims to the primary one of achieving a technically satisfactory result. He therefore should not be preoccupied with making his solutions as "interesting" as those of Bach, but rather in absorbing from the latter what he is capable of learning regarding such matters as solidity of structure; smoothness, strength, and directness of harmonic movement; variety and relevant profile in the movement of the bass line; and, finally, logic and vitality in the inner voices.

Secondly, the student should keep constantly in mind the fact that each chorale of Bach is an individual work of art, with its own requirements and its own problems. He will find the chorales, viewed in this light, infinitely varied even on the most elementary technical level. He should observe always the connections between the means used and the effect produced, and should note Bach's constant preoccupation with the sense of the text and his infinite resourcefulness in underlining it, sometimes in a generalized, sometimes in a very specific, sense — even in certain cases emphasizing one or the other of its aspects in the light of a larger context: e.g., a cantata, motet, or oratorio. Provided that the student keeps his primary technical aim uppermost in his mind, he can enlarge and refine his resources by such observations, and achieve results which will be of great value to him in quite other contexts.

In harmonizing chorales, the student should first of all carefully plan his cadences, as indicated by the *fermate* in the text. These are the points which bear the greatest harmonic weight, being the harmonic goals of the various phrases, and it is necessary to conceive them in such a manner that they form a consistent harmonic plan — one which contributes both solidity to the tonal structure, by enhancing the feeling of the key, and movement, through variety. The modulations studied in this section will form the basis of the tonal framework; in terms of the larger structure of the chorale, they may be considered very precisely as modulations to the various degrees within a single larger key.

In the first chorale melodies given below, the cadence harmonies are indicated; they may be taken as models for those which follow.

In general, it will be advisable to end one of the first two phrases on the tonic harmony. Very frequently the structure of the melody will be such that these first two phrases form a single unit of two complementary parts. In the chorale "*Christus der ist mein Leben*," for instance, both of the first two phrases end on the third degree; the first ends on a weak beat, the second on a strong one, which gives the second phrase a more conclusive character. In the chorale "*Nun danket alle Gott*" this rhythmic pattern is reversed, but the phrases are bound together by the fact that the first phrase ends on the fifth degree of the scale, the second on the tonic.

Such facts will necessarily affect the choice of harmonies, but no rules can be given which will effectively govern this choice. It is necessary rather to learn through observation, trial and error, with Bach at hand as a guide.

Generally speaking, the phrases toward the middle of the chorale will end on harmonies other than the tonic; but if a strong cadence on the subdominant or the second degree occurs, it will be found most often — as, for instance, in the chorale "*Nun danket alle Gott*" — at the end of the next to the last phrase.

The essential harmonic movement of each phrase is the movement from one cadence to the next. Aside from the beginning, which will be most often on the tonic harmony — frequently repeated over the bar line — the movement should be conceived as proceeding smoothly from one cadence to the next. The choice of the first harmony of each phrase will be governed in part by its relationship to the harmony of the cadence immediately preceding. If the latter is a half cadence, the former will frequently — though by no means invariably — be the chord of resolution. From this point (the beginning of the phrase) the harmonies should be conceived in terms of the cadence toward which they are proceeding, and must move toward it as a goal.

The line of the bass is, of course, of the utmost importance, and the greatest attention should be given to its construction.

Exercises

Harmonization of chorales, with cadences figured.

V   VI   I

Nun danket alle Gott

(3)

I   I
or V

V   V

IV   I

Jesu, meine Freude

(4)

I   V

I   III

V   I

O Ewigkeit, du Donnerwort

(5)

I

V   I

II   I

Freu' dich sehr, O meine Seele

(6)

Herr, ich habe missgehandelt

(7)

Valet will ich dir geben

(8)

Harmonization of chorales (unfigured).

Ach, wie nichtig

(9)

Vater unser in Himmelreich

(10)

Ermunt're dich mein, schwacher Geist

(11)

Wachet auf

(12)

Jesu, Leiden, Pein, und Tod

(13)

Ach, Gott und Herr

(14)

Die Sonn' hat sich

(15)

Wenn mein' Stundelein

(16)

Herzlich tut mich Verlangen

(17)

Nun komm, der Heiden Heiland

(18)

Dir, Dir, Jehova, will ich Singen

(19)

Christ lag in Todesbanden

(20)

CHAPTER

TEN

Modal Alterations

1. "MIXED" MODES

The resources of both the major and the minor modes are very frequently extended by the use in either of the two modes of tones and harmonies from the other. The most obvious instances of this process, of course, are those which result from the use of altered tones in the minor mode, or on the other hand, the custom, prevalent even as late as the time of Bach, of ending compositions in the minor mode with a major triad — the so-called "*tierce de Picardie*" (Picardy third).

As has already been noted (pp. 24, 42, 61, 104 ff.), the minor mode in its general usage is a mixture of minor and major elements, and in practice is rarely found in its "pure," that is, its most consistently "minor," form. The demands of tonality and tonal structure, ever since composers began to be aware of them, have given the minor mode an inherently mixed quality; and composers have made full use of the resources yielded by this quality. By so utilizing these resources they have extended them not only within the minor mode itself, but in the major mode as well.

Without a clear understanding of this fact, it is impossible to understand the harmonic facts which form the basis of the musical language and technique of Mozart and Haydn, or even, in a more detailed sense, the musical language of Bach. In the work of these composers, and of all later composers, are to be found many instances of the most daring application of mixed-mode principles, and many passages which are frequently though inaccurately cited as instances of deliberate tonal vagueness (for example, the often cited opening of Mozart's *Quartet in C Major* (K. 465), or the opening of Beethoven's *Quartet No. 9* (Op. 59, No. 3), in the same key) become quite clear when understood in these terms.

In the Mozart instance, harmonies borrowed from c minor are mingled with some major elements to prepare and elaborate a dominant which then leads to the main body of the movement in an unequivocal C major. The Beethoven instance may be generally characterized in the same terms. Harmonically and rhythmically it is the more elaborate of the two, but the two passages are, in spite of their obvious differences, actually quite similar in structure and function, the basis of the progression in each case being the downward scalewise movement — which is chromatically elaborated at times — of the violoncello part.

2. MINOR RELATIONSHIPS IN THE MAJOR MODE

The most frequent instance of this procedure in the major mode is the use of harmonies involving the minor sixth: IV_b, II_{b5}, and — somewhat more drastic in effect, since it involves alteration of the third as well — $\flat VI_{b5}$.

FIG. 171

The figuration used here (IV♭, etc.) is applicable in C major, as well as the simpler flat keys (F, B♭, E♭). When applied to other keys, the appropriate figuration must be used (e.g., in G, the minor seventh is ♮VII; in A♭, the lowered second is ♭♭II).

The use of ♭III involves the alteration of the major third, a more drastic departure from the major mode; therefore, somewhat more care is required if awkward or illogical progressions are to be avoided. If the seventh remains unaltered, an augmented triad, of course, results.

♭VII and v♭ involve the alteration of the leading tone, which even in the minor mode most frequently takes the form of the major seventh. v♭ is perhaps most frequently found in connection with the tonicization of II; but both harmonies may be used also — since the minor seventh does not, like the sixth or the third, imply a vivid contrast in mode — in connection with other harmonies, e.g.:

FIG. 172

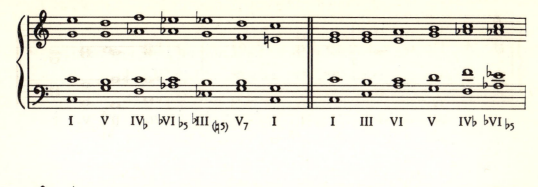

FIG. 173

Finally, ♭II is frequently introduced into the major mode.

The above examples illustrate the most logical application of the principles involved here: chromatic movement is avoided, and the altered harmonies are used strictly in accordance with their usage in the minor mode proper.

Although such strict application precludes chromatic movement in the voices, the latter is nevertheless possible, provided the outer voices be led in such a way as to justify such movement. It is, once again, impossible to provide directions for achieving good results, but, in the beginning, it may be found helpful to keep in mind the fact that a line progressing chromatically continues most logically in the direction of the alteration, e.g.:

FIG. 174

3. CROSS RELATIONS

Care must also be taken in the matter of "*cross relations*" — i.e., instances in which an altered note in one voice occurs just before or just after the same note, unaltered, in another voice, either in the same or a different octave, e.g.:

FIG. 175

Cross relations will be found awkward only when they have no clear motivation in the melodic, harmonic, or rhythmic design. Though they are sometimes forbidden or at least restricted to specific instances, it is actually impossible, in this case too, to establish rules regarding their use. The student must learn to be aware of them, and to use them only with intent; but above all he must learn to avoid irrelevancies of any kind, and to be sure that he is always producing the actual effect which he intends. The main principles involved at this point are that (1) each altered note should have a clear destination — or, in other terms, no note should be altered except in the interests of a clear harmonic direction — and (2) on every scale — i.e., either in detail or in matters of larger design — a given progression, harmonic or melodic, should reach its goal before the direction of the movement is changed. This will in nearly all cases involve stepwise motion away from the altered note, since by this means the direction becomes clearest. The following examples should help to clarify this point:

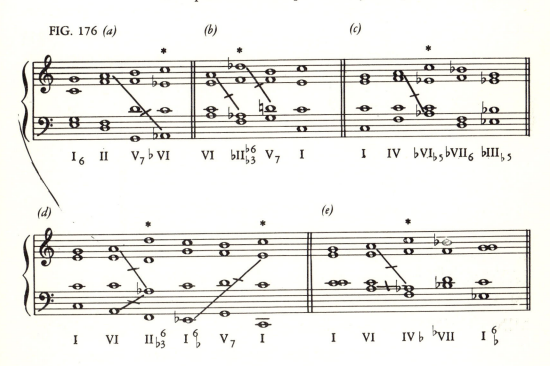

FIG. 176 (a)   (b)   (c)

(d)   (e)

* See following paragraph.

While in Figure 176 (a) the harmonic situation is very clear and the cross relation therefore quite unproblematical, the other instances are much more problematical, since they involve more violent and apparently unmotivated juxtapositions of altered and unaltered notes. The impossibility of making rules, however, may be understood more clearly if the starred chords are considered in each case as strongly accented. Any detail which brings a high degree of contrast or surprise will be inevitably thrown into strong relief; it must therefore coincide with a very strong rhythmic, metrical, or expressive accent. If no such accent is intended or provided by the context, such a detail will inevitably seem awkward and even "false."

Contrast, in other words, implies accent, and the degree of contrast must correspond with the desired intensity of accentuation. The converse, of course, is also true: accent demands a requisite degree of contrast. Many of the commonest faults in harmonic writing may be traced ultimately to violation — generally through unawareness — of this principle, and to the disproportion of effect which results therefrom. The principle is subtle in its application, however, and impossible to reduce, even on the simplest level, to any kind of formula.

4. MAJOR RELATIONSHIPS IN THE MINOR MODE

The altered sixth and seventh degrees in the minor mode have already been defined as "borrowed" — for strictly functional purposes — from the major mode. Even in this functional sense they may now be used somewhat more freely than before.

For example, the tonic may descend toward the dominant by way of the altered seventh and sixth degrees.

FIG. 177

$I_{\sharp 7}$, hitherto unused except in the form of a "frozen" seventh (p. 229), is now perfectly possible in such contexts as the following:

FIG. 178

The augmented second formed by the minor sixth and major seventh may be used if this is done with express melodic intent — that is, when the augmented second is wanted for its own sake.

FIG. 179

BEETHOVEN, *Quartet in C-sharp Minor*, Op. 131

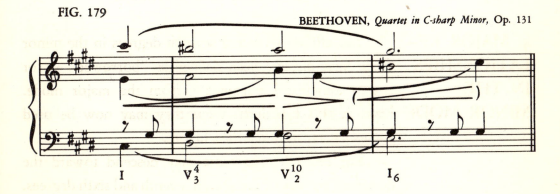

It will be easily seen that these still comparatively restricted uses of the altered sixth and seventh in the minor mode do not really correspond with the uses of minor harmonies in a prevailing major mode (pp. 287 ff.). In a fairly rough sense it may be observed that while, in the minor mode, the altered harmonies actually strengthen the tonic-dominant relationship by means of the raised seventh, the introduction of harmonies borrowed from the minor mode into a prevailing major mode fulfills a quite different function — in a general sense, that of providing more resources of contrast and therefore of expression.

Similar devices may be used in the minor mode also, not only with the chords already familiar, e.g.:

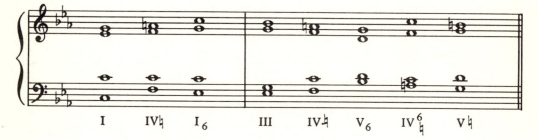

but above all with chords involving the major triad.

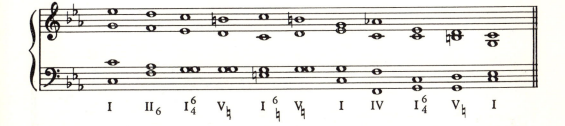

While, in the major mode, the major seventh (in a seventh chord) will be frequently altered in accordance with the procedure described in this chapter:

FIG. 182

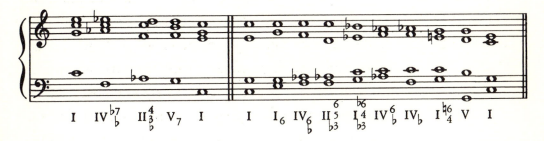

the converse procedure is rarer in the minor mode, for the obvious reason that the seventh, in its original sense as described in Chapter Six, moves *downward*, while a tone which is chromatically raised tends generally *upward*. Such alterations of the seventh (starred below) will not occur, therefore, unless the major mode is temporarily very well established, as in the following:

FIG. 183

5. ARCHAISTIC AND EXOTIC VARIANTS

The procedures described in this chapter provide one of the keys to the use, in the music of the nineteenth and twentieth centuries, of such archaistic or exotic devices as the "church modes" and the exotic or "local" scales which are used from time to time for various types of "special effect." When employed by composers of the Occidental tradition, such development must be considered as the "posttonal" application of procedures which were, speaking generally, "pretonal" in origin, whether the term "pretonal" be understood in a historical or in a primitivistic sense. In other words, they appear in Western music fundamentally as variants or, if one will, as offshoots of a musical culture — a type of *musical ear* — which has tonality as its point of departure, however radical the departure may be.

Archaistic or exotic scales of a generally diatonic character may therefore be described as fixed or stylized patterns of modal alteration, and need no special treatment at this point. The interested student will find it quite easy to investigate them — and other such possibilities — for himself, and will find no difficulties in their use, provided he has mastered the procedures treated in this section.

Exercises

Figures only.

1. D $\text{I}-\text{II}_6-\text{II}^{\#6}_{4\ 3}-\text{V}-\text{II}^6_5-\text{I}_6-\text{IV}^6_{\flat}-\text{I}^{\natural 6}_4-\text{V}-\text{I}_\#$

2. f $\text{I}-\text{V}_6-\text{IV}_6-\text{V}^7_\natural-\natural\text{VI}-\text{II}^6_\natural-\natural\text{VII}_6-\flat\text{VI}-\flat\text{II}_6-\text{V}^7_\natural\ \text{I}$

3. B♭ $\text{I}-\text{IV}^6_\flat-\text{I}^6_4-\text{II}^6_{5\ \flat}-\text{I}^6_\flat-\text{II}^7_{\natural 5}-\text{V}_7-\text{I}$

4. c♯ $\text{I}-\text{I}_6-\text{IV}-\text{VII}^{\#4}_3-\text{I}^6_\#-\text{II}^7_{\#5}-\text{V}^7_\#-(\natural)\text{VI}-\text{IV}-\#\text{VII}_7-\text{I}$

5. E $\text{I VII}_6-\text{I}_6-\text{IV}_\natural-\natural\text{VI}-\natural\text{III}-\text{IV}^6_\natural-\text{I}^{\#6}_4-\text{V}-\text{I}$

6. g $\text{I IV}^4_3-\text{V}^6_\#-\text{II}^{\#6}_{4\ 3\ \natural}-\text{V}_\#-\#\text{IV}^6_\natural-\text{V}^6_\#-\text{VI}_6-\text{III}_{\#5}-\text{VI}-\flat\text{II}-\text{V}_{8-7}-\text{I}$

7. A♭ $\text{I}-\text{IV}^{\flat 7}_\flat-\text{VII}^2_{\flat}-(\natural)\text{III}_6-\flat\flat\text{II}^6_{\natural 3}-\text{V}^{(\natural)6}_2-\text{I}_6-\flat\text{VI}^6_4-\text{II}^7_\flat-\text{V}-\text{I}^6_{\flat 5}-\text{IV}_\flat-\text{I}^{(\natural)6}_4-\text{V}-\text{I}$

8. b $\text{I}-\text{VI}-\#\text{VII}_7-\text{I}_\#-\text{IV}_6-\natural\text{VII}-\text{II}_{\#5}-\text{III}^6_\#-\text{II}^6_{\natural 3}-\text{I}^6_\#-\#\text{IV}^6_\#-\text{I}^{(\natural)6}_4-\text{V}_7-\text{I}$

9. F $\text{I}-\text{II}^6_\flat-\text{I}_6-\natural\text{IV}_6-\text{V}-\flat\text{VI}-\text{I}^6_{(\natural)}-\flat\text{VII}^7_{6\ (\flat 5)\ 3}-\text{II}^6_5-\flat\text{I}_6-\flat\text{II}-\text{V}_7-\text{I}$

10. g♯ $\text{I}-\text{V}_\#-\text{III}-\#\text{VI}_6-\text{V}-\text{VII}_6-\text{II}_{\#5}-\text{III}_\ast-\#\text{VI}_6-\text{V}-\text{I}$

11. A $\text{I}-\text{VI}-\text{V}_\natural-\text{IV}^6_{\natural 5}-\natural\text{III}_{(\#5)}-\text{V}_7-\text{VII}_{\natural 7}-\natural\text{I}-\natural\text{VI}-\flat\text{II}^7_{(\natural 5)}-\text{V}_7-\text{I}$

12. e $\text{I}-\text{III}_{\#5}-\text{VI}-\text{I}^{\#6}_4-\#\text{VII}^4_{3\ \natural}-\text{I}^6_\#-\natural\text{VI}^6_4-\text{IV}^{\#4}_{\#2}-\text{V}^{\#6}_{4\ 3}-\text{I}_{(\natural)}-\natural\text{II}_6-\#\text{IV}_{\#7}-\#\text{IV}^{\#6}_{\natural 5}-\text{I}^{\natural 6}_4-\text{V}_7-\text{I}$

Figured basses.

Outer voices given, no chords indicated.

Vivace molto

Andante con moto

(2)

Andante

(3)

Moderato

(4)

Lento

(5)

Allegretto

(6)

Soprano voice, no chords indicated.

(2) Allegretto

(3) Adagio

(4) Moderato

CHAPTER

ELEVEN

Modulation (II)

1. MODULATION THROUGH MODAL ALTERATIONS

The combined resources of the major and minor modes now include the following harmonies:

FIG. 184

I Ib bII IIb♮ II bIII(b5) bIII♮5 III IV IVb V V bVI(b5) VIb5 VI bVII VII

As a result, the resources for modulation are enormously extended:

1. A chord which is altered in respect to the key of departure may become the pivot, through its function as an unaltered chord in the key of destination:

FIG. 185

C I V IVb   C I II⁶₅
  Eb II II₆ I II₆ V I   f (V) VI⁶₅ VII I₆ II⁶₅ V I

C I VII₆ VI⁶♭

B♭ VII₆ I₆ IV I⁶₄ V₇ I

C I IV⁶♭

A♭ VI₆ V₆ IV₆ I⁶₄ II₆ V I

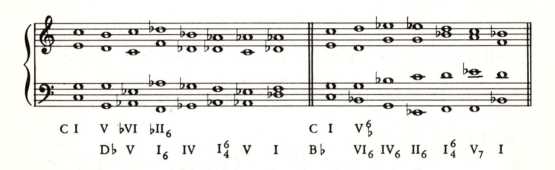

C I V ♭VI ♭II₆

D♭ V I₆ IV I⁶₄ V I

C I V⁶♭

B♭ VI₆ IV₆ II₆ I⁶₄ V₇ I

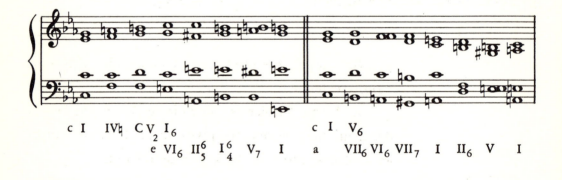

c I IV♮ C V₂ I₆

e VI₆ II⁶₅ I⁶₄ V₇ I

c I V₆

a VII₆ VI₆ VII₇ I II₆ V I

c I V₆

d IV⁶ V⁶₅ I VI II⁶₅ V I

In order to avoid unnecessarily complicated notation, enharmonic changes (see p. 18) will sometimes be
found advisable and even necessary:

FIG. 186

2. Conversely, an unaltered chord may assume the
function of an altered chord in the key of destination:

FIG. 187

C   I   V   III   C   I   IV   V₂   I₆
         b IV   V   B I   b ♮III₆   V   B I

c   I   IV₇   c   I   V
    f I₇ ♮VII⁶₅ F I   IV   I⁶₄   V   I   d IV D I⁶₄   V₇   I

3. An altered chord may become an altered chord in the key of destination by a shift of degree:

FIG. 188

C   I   I²♭ c IV₆   C   I   c IV⁶₄   VI₆
    b♭ V₆   IV₆ B♭ I⁶₄   V₇   I   f III₆   VI F I   V   I

C   I   c VII₆ III   c   I   II₂   V⁶₅ C   I
    g VI   II   I⁶₄   V   I   a III   V   I   IV₆   V   I

c I   IVᵇ ᵇVII₆ C I₆
    G IV₆ #VII₇   I   II⁶₅ V   I

2. SEQUENCES: TONICIZED PIVOT: CIRCLE OF FIFTHS

Three further extensions of modulation are as follows:

4. Modulation may be effected through the sequential repetition of a harmonic pattern, often involving secondary dominant or leading-tone harmonies:

FIG. 189

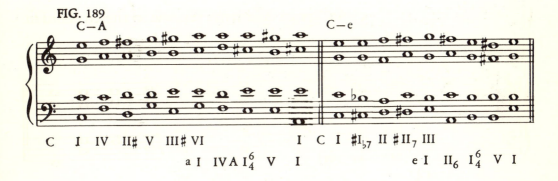

C I IV II# V III# VI   I C I #I♭₇ II #II₇ III
        a I IVA I⁶₄ V   I   e I II₆ I⁶₄ V I

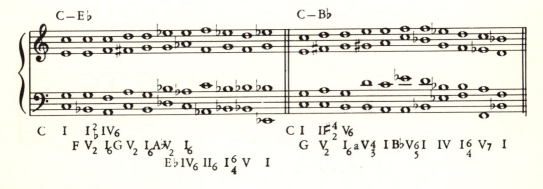

C I I♭²₃IV₆   C I IF#⁴₂ V₆
    F V₂ I₆G V₂ I₆A V₂ I₆   G V₂ I₆ a V⁴₃ I B♭V₆₅I IV I⁶₄ V₇ I
        E♭IV₆ II₆ I⁶₄ V I

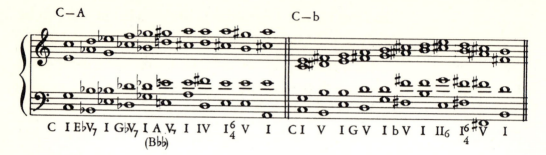

C I E♭V₇ I G♭V₇ I A V₇ I IV I⁶₄ V I   C I V I G V I b V I II₆ I⁶₄ #V I
(B♭♭)

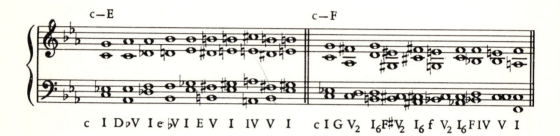

c I D♭V I e♭VI E V I IV V I   c I G V₂ I₆F#V₂ I₆ f V₂ I₆F IV V I

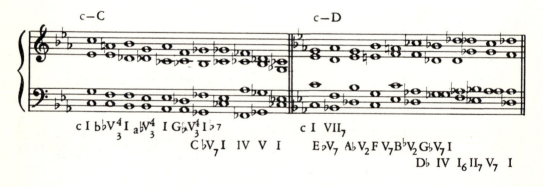

c I b♭V⁴₃ I a♭V⁴₃ I G♭V⁴₃ I♭⁷   c I VII₇
C ♭V₇ I IV V I   E♭V₇ A♭V₂ F V₇ B♭V₂ G♭V₇ I
D♭ IV I₆ II₇ V₇ I

The effect of such a modulation will depend on ·(1) the simplicity of the pattern involved, (2) the relationship of the keys at each end, and (3) the regularity of the harmonic path along which the pattern moves. A pattern which is too complex, or in which a single feature is too prominent, will not bear sequential repetition as well as a simpler one in which the ear is less arrested by detail (see p. 216); the more remote the relationship of the key of destination to that of departure, the more forced and mechanical a sequence is likely to be; in order to be fully convincing, a sequence must move by regular diatonic intervals (by seconds, by thirds, etc.) though not necessarily by absolutely symmetrical ones (i.e., by *major* seconds, or *minor* thirds, etc.).

5. A modulation to a distant key may often be made smoother and more convincing by strongly tonicizing the pivotal harmony, thus effecting the modulation in two stages, e.g.:

FIG. 190

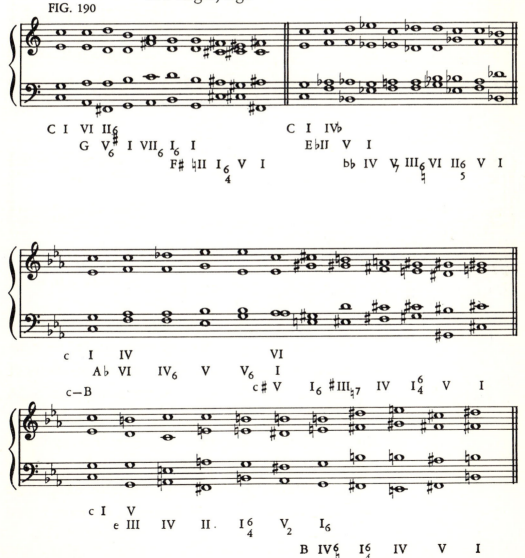

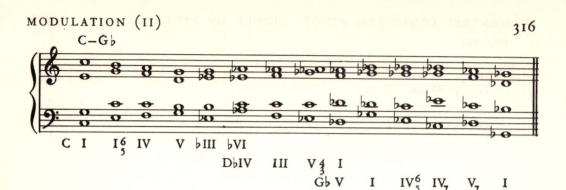

C–Gb

C   I   I$^6_5$ IV   V   bIII   bVI

Db IV   III   V$^4_3$ I

Gb V   I   IV$^6_5$ IV$_7$ V$_7$ I

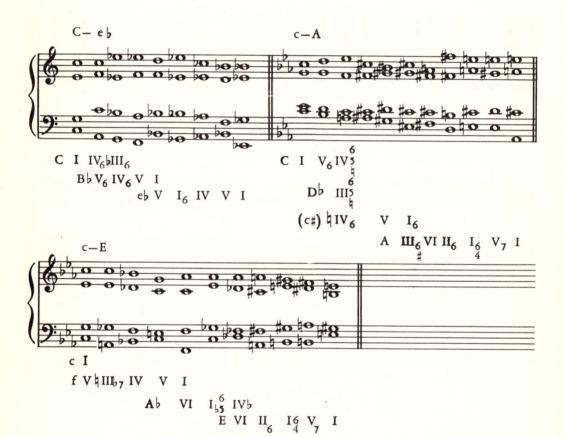

C– eb

C   I   IV$_6$ bIII$_6$

Bb V$_6$ IV$_6$ V   I

eb V   I$_6$ IV   V   I

c–A

C   I   V$_6$ IV$^6_5$$_\natural$

Db   III$_5$$^6_\natural$

(c#) $\natural$IV$_6$ V   I$_6$

A   III$_6$ VI   II$_6$ I$_6$ V$_7$ I
      $_\sharp$ $_4$

c–E

c   I

f   V $\natural$III$_{b7}$ IV   V   I

Ab   VI   I$^6_{b5}$ IVb

E   VI   II$_6$ I$^6_4$ V$_7$ I

6. Modulation may be effected by moving along the circle of fifths, either upward or downward. This movement generally continues one step beyond the key of destination, in order to create the necessary tonal balance.

If the movement is downward by fifths, various patterns involving secondary dominants (or substitute chords, pp. 228 ff., 243–248) are possible:

FIG. 192

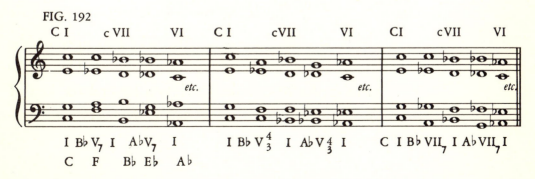

This includes the downward succession of dominant chords, which should descend to the subdominant triad of the key of destination (see pp. 257–258):

FIG. 193

C I V
of Eb Ab Bb DbI
Bb
Ab IV

C I V of F Bb Eb Ab Db Gb GbI I V I

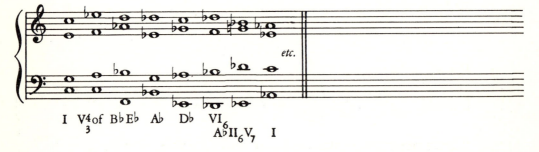

etc.

I V$\frac{4}{3}$of BbEb Ab Db VI$_6$
AbII$_6$V$_7$ I

In the following exercises, the student should bear in mind the linear aspect of the sequence (p. 219).

Exercises

Figures only.

1. B I–II$_7$–III$_{\natural5}^{\natural7}$–IV$_\natural$ = D II–V$_6$–I$_6$–V–I
2. " " " " " = d II$_{\natural5}$–VII$_6$–I$_6$–II$_5^6$–V–I
3. " " " " " = C III–II–I$_4^6$–V$_7$–I
4. " " " " " = c $\natural$III–I$_4^{\natural6}$–$\flat$II$_6$–I$_4^6$–V$_7$–I
   3
5. " " " " " = a V$_\natural$–IV$_6$–IV–V–I
6. " " " " " = A V$_\natural$–IV$_\natural^6$–V$_{(\sharp)}^6$–V$_3^4$–I
7. " " " " " = G VI–II$_6$–V$_7$–I

8. " " " " " $=$ g ♮VI–IV♮–VII#6–VI6–IV6–I$^6_4$–V–I

9. " " " " " $=$ F VII♮–V$^6_{♭5}$–I–II$^6_5$–I$^6_4$–V$_7$–I

10. " " " " " $=$ f ♮VII♮5–♮VII $^{6}_{5\,♭3}$–I6–II$^6_5$–V$_7$–I

11. g I–III–IV–V#–IV♮^{6} $=$ e VI6–#VII$^6_5$–I6–IV–V–I

12. " " " " " " $=$ E ♮VI6–V2–I$^6_{♮4}$–IV♮^{6}–I$^6_4$–V$_7$–I

13. f I–III–IV♮^{6}–♮VI$^6_{♮3}$ $=$ a IV6–I6–II$_7$–V–I

14. " " " " " $=$ C II6–V$_7$–I

15. " " " " " $=$ B♭ III6–V$^4_3$–I$_{♭,}$–♮IV$_{♭,7}$–V–I

16. " " " " " $=$ g V6–IV6–I$^6_4$–V–I

17. " " " " " $=$ A IV♮^{6}–I$^6_4$–V$_7$–I

18. A I–♮VII6 $=$ F# ♮II6–V–VI–II$^6_5$–V$_7$–I

19. b♭ I–IV6–V–II♮^{6} $=$ A♭ III$_{♭6}$ $=$ g#: IV6–IV–I$^6_4$–V–I
 (a♭)

20. " " " " " $=$ g IV6–#IV♮^{7}–I$^6_4$–V$_7$–I

21. E I–V6 $=$ d# VI6–V$^6_5$; E♭ I–II$^6_5$–V–I
 (e♭)

22. " " " $=$ c# VII6; C# VI$^6_5$–II–I6–V$_{8-7}$–I
 (#)

23. " " " $=$ a# ♮II6; B♭ V2–I6–II$_7$–I$^6_4$–V$_7$–I
 (b♭)

24. E I–V6–♮VI6 $=$ g IV♮^{6}–VII$_7$–I–II6–V$_7$–I

25. d I–VII6–I6 $=$ B♭ III6–V$^6_5$–I $\left[\begin{array}{l} = \text{B VII}^{#5}_{✕3} \\ (\text{v of III}) \end{array}\right]$; B V$^6_5$–I–II$^6_5$–V–I

26. C I–V$^6_{♭,}$ $=$ d IV6–V–I $\left[\begin{array}{l} = \text{E♭ VII}_{♮5} \\ (\text{e♭ ♮VII}_{♮5}) \end{array}\right]$; e♭ II$^{♮5}_{♮3}$–V–VI–II$^6_5$–V–I

27. g I–III$^4_{♭,3}$–VI $=$ A♭ V–V$^6_5$–I (= E III#); E VI–II$^4_3$–I$^6_4$–V$_7$–I

28. D♭ I–V6–♮I,$_7$–II (= B III); B I6–II$_7$–V$^4_3$–I (= G III#); G IV–II$_7$–V$_7$–I

29. f# I–V♮^{6}–VI (= F VI#); F I$^4_{♭,3}$–IV–V–I6 (= C# III✕6); c# VI–IV–II–I$^6_4$–V$_7$–I

30. A♭ I–IV (= B II#); B V–I6–IV–VII6–I (= c# VII); c# II$^4_3$–III$^6_#$–IV–I$^6_4$–V–I

31. b I–V$^6_#$–#VI6–#VII6–#I6 (= F# #IV6); F# V–I–IV (= A II$^#_#$);
 A I6–II6–I$^6_4$–V–I.

32. E♭ I–V6–♭VI$^6_{♮3}$ (= C♭ I$^6_{♮3}$); C♭ II6–V$_7$–I (= E v); E II6–VI$^6_4$–I6–II$_7$–V$_7$–I

Make the following modulations, using different sequential patterns.

1. D–B♭	5. E–C	9. E♭–B (C♭)
2. f–C	6. b♭–d	10. g–b
3. A♭–D♭	7. G♭–A	11. A–f
4. f♯–B♭ (A♯)	8. d–b	12. c♯–F

Make each of the following modulations three times, making use each time of a different pivotal key.

13. B–f	16. e–b♭	19. E–f
14. a–A♭	17. C♯–E♭	20. c–b
15. D♭–D	18. d♯–c♯	

The same principles may be applied also to keys which are more closely related, for the purpose not of smoothness but of contrast. The following exercises, in which the intermediate key is given, will illustrate this procedure.

21. C–A♭–G	24. g–e–C	27. F–E–a
22. b–E♭–G	25. D♭–a–f	28. E♭–D♭–B♭
23. A–f–d	26. g♯–a–E	

The foregoing are intended merely as samples. At this point in harmonic study, intensive experimentation is of the utmost importance. The possibilities are so vast that they cannot be adequately systematized or tabulated in any useful form. The student, by working out similar exercises of his own conception, can gain a sharper feeling for the relationships between keys.

Soprano voice, modulations indicated.

Andante

(2)

A I

aIV   (VI₆)

Allegro moderato

(3)

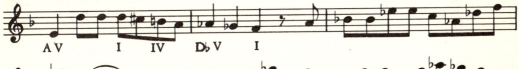

f V   Gb I   (f♯)

A V   I   IV   Db V   I

I= f VI   F V

Adagio

(4)

III   G V

II×   I₆
(V of V)

Moderato

(5)

A I

B♭ I

D I

g I (B♭ IV)

Lento

(6)

A♭ I

Allegro

(7)

C I

F I

G I

Andante

(8)

Allegretto

(9)

Lento

(10)

Soprano voice, no chords indicated.

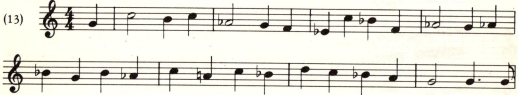

Allegro moderato

(14)

Allegro

(15)

Lento

(19)

Andante

(20)

CHAPTER

TWELVE

Introduction to
Chromatic Harmony

1. PRINCIPLES OF CHROMATIC ALTERATION

A tone may be chromatically altered in order to produce either of the following effects:

(1) By raising or lowering it chromatically, it may be brought closer to the tone which, in any given progression, immediately follows;

(2) By lowering or raising the first of two repeated tones, contrast may be introduced into an otherwise momentarily static line.

This is, of course, an extension to the chromatic sphere of the principle described in pages 224–231. Thus, for example:

FIG. 194

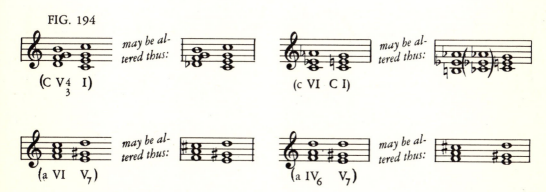

(F V   I)   (C III   I)   etc.
                    (e I   VI)

This principle may be applied to more than one voice at the same time, e.g.:

FIG. 195

may be altered to:

(C VII$_7$ I)

(a II$_2$ V$_5^6$)   (a II$_3^4$ V$_7$)

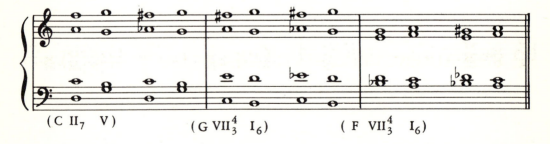

(C II$_7$ V)   (G VII$_3^4$ I$_6$)   (F VII$_3^4$ I$_6$)

* Cf. Mozart, *Symphony in G Minor* (K. 550), first movement, measures 150, 152.

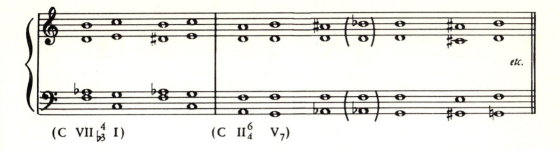

$(C\ VII{}^{4}_{\flat 3}\ I)$ $(C\ II{}^{6}_{4}\ V_7)$

It will be seen immediately that very drastic contrasts may be produced in this manner. Not all of them will be immediately useful, and the ear and taste of the student must guide him in their use. He should, at first, however, explore the possibilities as fully as possible, in accordance with the following sample exercises.

Exercises

Modify, through chromatic alteration, the following progressions in as many different ways as possible, using a different major and then a different minor key for each progression.

1. II–V	6. II^6_5–V	11. IV_6–V
2. III–I	7. VII^4_3–III	12. II^4_3–V
3. IV–VI	8. VI_7–VII	13. III^4_3–IV_6
4. I–II	9. VII_2–I^6_4	14. II_7–I_6
5. I^4_3–IV	10. II^6_5–I	15. VI_7–V^6_5

2. THE AUGMENTED SIXTH CHORDS

The principle of alteration has produced various chordal types which have long been in general use and which are universally considered as "standard" chords.

Chief among these are the *"augmented sixth chords,"* classified as *"Italian," "French,"* and *"German":*

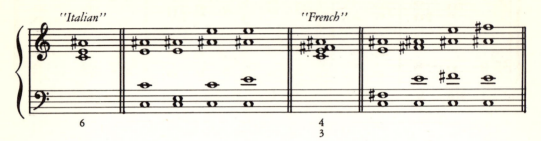

The augmented sixth chords are generally considered to have originated as modifications of the subdominant harmony, or of the harmony of the second degree in the minor mode. According to this concept, the above would be figured respectively as $\sharp IV_6$, $II^{\sharp 6}_4$, $\sharp IV^6_5$, in e minor; and $\maltese II^{\sharp 6}_{(\maltese)4}$, in E major, resolving normally as follows:

FIG. 196

$\sharp IV_6$ V $II\,^{\sharp 6}_{4}$ V $\sharp IV^6_5$ I^6_4 V $\times II\,^{\sharp 6}_{4}$ I^6_4 V
                                3   .3
                                                                               ♮

Vertical and horizontal implications

The above figuration is adopted here for convenience' sake. In practice, these chords (see Fig. 197) have such varying usages that their harmonic sense must be considered as varying also. Discussions about the "real root" of chords may thus be considered, not so much as discussions of the nature of the chords, but rather as points which have really to do with the larger theoretical question of the meaning of roots and of root progression. The author holds strongly to the view that root progression is a concrete and observable fact, not a question simply of theoretical interpretation and analysis, and that it has its basis in the intervallic relationships described in pages 72–77. In other words, root progression is in essence a musical effect or *sensation*, and the theoretical concept, here as elsewhere, has meaning only when it more or less adequately covers the essential musical fact — when the sensation, in other words, is clear and unequivocal.

In a subtler sense, root progression may be conceived as an *impulse* which is very frequently the decisive element in the relationship between chords, and especially so at those points which carry the strongest rhythmic or accentual weight — cadences, climaxes, etc. As has already been pointed out under the topic "Harmonic Elaboration" (pp. 200 ff.), a chord may, according to its context, result from either a contrapuntal or a harmonic impulse: that is, from either the impulse inherent in voice leading or that inherent in root progression.

It is clear that the process of alteration, like that described under the topic "Frozen Accessory Tones" (pp. 224 ff.), brings new elements into the picture. The alterations which produce secondary dominant chords, or such other chords as further the process of tonicization (pp. 243 ff.), have of course the effect of strengthening the sense of root progression. This is in fact the essence of tonicization, since the progression toward a tonic, especially from a dominant, is root progression in its strongest, even in its archetypal, form.

In other cases, an alteration will support the actual root progression by the addition of a linear element (pp. 32–33, 206, 213, 219), which, though essentially extraneous to the root progression, is nowise in conflict with it. In the progression below

C   V$^7_{\sharp 5}$ I

for instance, the alteration of D to D♯ increases the "pull" of the seventh chord, without either confirming or disturbing the sense of the relationship G–C which is the root relationship involved. The "pull" of the D♯ toward the note E involves a single voice only, and has the effect of bringing the latter — the doubled third — into heightened relief.

In still other cases, the linear "pull" of the alteration has become so strong as to take precedence over the effect of root relationship and to call into question the relevance of the latter. In such cases, the alteration has lost the character of a single instance and become a typical one — the chord has become so typical and so general in its usage that it has won an independent and recognizable existence and has been applied to a variety of situations, not on the basis of its "root," but of the principle of the alteration as such.

This is underlined sharply in the case of the augmented sixth chords. Their very definition as such runs counter to the idea of root progression, since it accentuates the fact that it is the characteristic augmented interval with its tendency to resolve outward, rather than a "root," which gives the chord its character and its reason for existence. It is the position of the sixth, therefore, not the "root" position, which is considered as fundamental. This is not — as in the case of the "Neapolitan" sixth chord (p. 114) — simply because the position of the sixth is most usual, but because it embodies to the highest degree the actual usage of the chord, since the characteristic interval of the chord here has the lowest voice as its lowest tone. It is not the "root" movement but the augmented interval that gives the chord its character.

Variants of the augmented sixth

The harmonic sense of the augmented sixth chord varies with the context. As the following table shows, resolutions quite other than the above are possible; other tones than the (augmented) sixth of the chord may be used with the sense of altered tones, and in some cases (Ex. a, b, c, d, j, m, and more especially q) it is not the sixth at all, but one or more of the other tones, which are the alterations. In most of these cases the concept of root progression is still possible, though in some cases (notably Ex. m) the pull of the voices is so much stronger and more perceptible than that of the root progression that the question of the latter seems purely academic. The resolutions of the examples in the table, while doubtless less frequently to be found than those cited above (pp. 331–333), are nevertheless all quite possible; the student may also find others. The figurations given in parentheses for each chord represent the author's interpretation in terms of root progression *as heard;* in some cases this corresponds to the literal shape of the chord as expressed in the notation, while in others the altered note is to be considered as an "added" sixth (see pp. 228–229) and the chord is interpreted accordingly.

FIG. 197

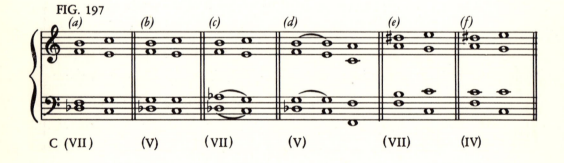

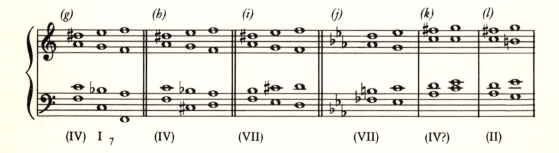

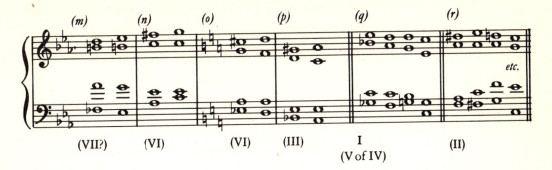

Still other positions (or inversions) of the same chord are frequently to be found:

Exercise

Work out as many resolutions as possible for each of the chords indicated in Figures 197 and 198. Use different positions (i.e., distributions of the voices), in four-part harmony. The resolutions given for the augmented sixth chords (pp. 331–333) may be used as models — the same resolutions being applied to the respective inversions — e.g.:

FIG. 199

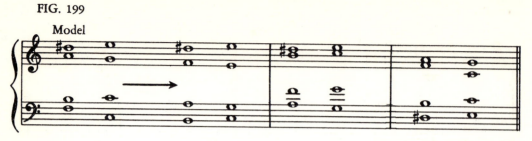

Model

but the student should try also to find other resolutions along the same lines applied here — i.e., considering under what circumstances each of the various tones can be regarded as altered.

The remarks on page 198, in regard to consecutive fifths resulting from the use of accessory tones, are even more applicable in the case of those which result from altered tones. When the sense of the altered tones is quite clear, the effect of the fifths may be considered quite harmless. When the student — as should certainly be the case at this point — has attained a degree of ease and security in handling consecutive fifths, he may safely be left to his own judgment in this respect. It will also be found that in positions in which the augmented sixth is inverted (as always in the positions under (a) in Fig. 198) the diminished third should if possible be used in a compound form (9th or 16th), preferably with another voice between.

FIG. 200

sometimes of good effect

and even

generally preferable to:

etc.

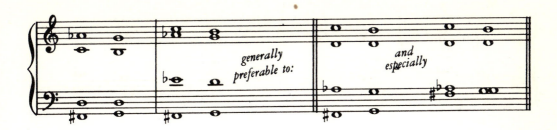

3. SOME ALTERATIONS OF TRIADS AND SEVENTH CHORDS

The following alterations may be derived from the triad (illustrated in the key of C).

FIG. 201

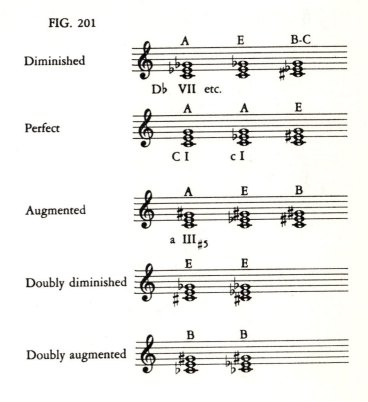

And the following may be derived from the seventh chord:

FIG. 202

The chords indicated in Figures 201 and 202 with an "A" are identical in structure with chords already familiar as degrees based on the diatonic scale. These are indicated in each case under the chord in question.

The chords indicated with a "B" are identical *in sound* with chords which are already familiar as regular harmonies in the diatonic scale, as may be seen if the notation is simplified through enharmonic change, e.g.:

FIG. 203

In these cases, as in those under "C," the notation results from the context in which the chord belongs — i.e., whether or not the chord is altered, and what is the direction of the altered note.

The "C" chords are "root" positions of the "French," "German," and "Italian" sixth chords (pp. 331–333). Since — a point presently to be discussed — the "Italian" and "German" sixth chords, if taken out of context, are undistinguishable in sound from the unaltered dominant seventh chord, the indication "B–C" identifies them.

Under "D" are chords containing the augmented sixth (or diminished third) but different in structure from those under "C." Of these, the chord with the major third is extremely familiar as an alteration of the dominant seventh chord, but it is also used in other contexts.

The letter "E" indicates chords which, though in varying degrees possible, and sometimes quite familiar, as individual instances of alteration, it has never seemed very necessary to classify in any generalized sense.

Any attempt at classification of altered chords is in certain respects arbitrary. It is the *process* and not the individual instance that is important, though the fact that certain alterations have through reiterated usage attained, so to speak, chordal dignity, is illustrative of a far-reaching process in musical development — a process which will be under discussion, direct or implied, for the rest of this volume. But, in the opinion of the author, the process is still very far from any adequate theoretical formulation.

4. ALTERATION AND ENHARMONIC CHANGE

By means of enharmonic change, the seventh chords listed in Figure 202 (a) may be rewritten to read as in Figure 202 (b).

These chords, with the exception of those formerly in category "A," are simpler in aspect than the chords in Figure 202 (a). To category "Aa" have been assigned chords whose structure readily places them among the chords classified as resulting from "frozen" accessory tones (pp. 224 ff.).

Of special interest is category "A" in Figure 202 (b). It contains not only the enharmonically altered chords hitherto classified under "B," but (1) the enharmonic alteration of the German sixth, which is thus shown to be undistinguishable, apart from its context, from the dominant seventh chord, and (2) the three inversions of the diminished seventh chord, all derived enharmonically from the same chord in its root position. The significance of these facts will be made clear in the next two sections of this chapter.

Category "B" has, of course, disappeared by the very process of enharmonic simplification.

Category "C" not only confirms, by a process of exchange, the identity of the German sixth and the dominant seventh chord, but draws attention to the structural identity of the French sixth and its second inversion.

To category "D" are added two new chords, both of them enharmonic alterations of chords familiar as "secondary sevenths," and both in very frequent use.

The above, of course, illustrates only a few of the possibilities resulting from enharmonic change. The major seventh chord, for instance, could in certain situations be enharmonically altered thus:

FIG. 204

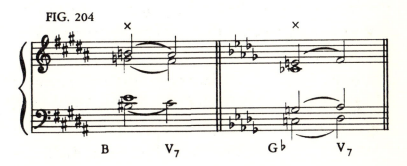

B   V₇   G♭   V₇

Even the major triad may be altered enharmonically:

FIG. 205

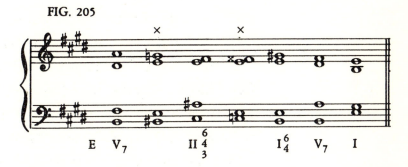

E   V₇   II 6/4/3   I 6/4   V₇   I

The above are by no means unusual in the music of the nineteenth century, and serve to illustrate still further the extent of the resources available.

Exercises

Using the exercise prescribed on page 337 as a model, work out as many resolutions as possible for the following.

Find two inversions and two enharmonically altered forms of each of the above chords, and lead each (again in accordance with the exercise on page 337) to as many different triads or seventh chords as possible.

Problems of figuration and notation

Since the principle of alteration runs actually counter to that of root progression as studied up to this point (see pp. 333–335) — a fact of which the musical consequences have been incalculable, and which will be discussed briefly in the final section of this work — Roman numerals are really irrelevant when applied to these altered chords, and have been omitted here except when directly useful for explanatory purposes.

The student will find also, as he progresses, that the facts illustrated by the two tables of seventh chords (Fig. 202) immediately raise questions of notation. Actually, composers have at all times avoided pedantry in this matter and have sought the simplest and most practical notation consistent with a reasonably clear picture of the musical sense. This practice has everything to recommend it; but the student should adopt it preferably by degrees, and very consciously. Simplified enharmonic notation may be regarded as a kind of recognition that a chord has become something more than an "alteration." In learning to use such chords, it is well to keep their original sense clearly in mind. It is therefore recommended that the simplest notation be adopted, in each case, only after the resolution has been worked out on the basis of the stricter form.

While the above remarks and exercises do not constitute an exhaustive summary of the resources yielded by the process of alteration, such a summary would actually be quite useless. The student will, through practice, discover the resources for himself. It is the *process* which is important, and the treatment of the subject given here is designed to give an understanding of this process and an introductory indication of the uses to which it may be put.

Nature of the new resources discussed

The nature of the new resources contributed by the technique of "alteration" should now be clear. By bridging the distances between notes, alteration brings new possibilities of *smoothness of movement*, and of *subtlety of contrast;* on the other hand, through the relationship of the semitone, it provides additional means of throwing single voices into momentary relief.

In a harmonic sense, "altered chords" fulfill a role analogous to that of the secondary dominants, but in even greater measure, owing to the heightened potency created by the "pull" of the altered note; by the stronger dissonantal contrast; and by the tonal contrast which results from the altered chord being, in its original sense, *in fact* "altered," and therefore relatively removed from the tonal center.

The "altered" chords, thus, already in themselves imply the sharp juxtaposition of greater tonal distances than have hitherto been brought into such close conjunction; with their use more "happens," harmonically, within a short space of time, and thus the whole harmonic profile is heightened in detail.

Caution regarding use of altered chords

It is customary at this point to warn the student against excessive use of altered notes and "altered chords"; and, indeed, alteration is a technique which has created many musical problems. More than any other single factor, perhaps, it has gone into the making of what is most characteristic in the music of the twentieth century, and has raised the questions to which the most gifted composers of today are seeking, and sometimes finding, their individual answers.

Certainly the serious student of compositional technique — whatever his ultimate aims — must learn to gain the technical control which can only come as the result of full awareness of every effect which he produces; and, to this end, he should proceed slowly at first, avoiding both the excessive use of alteration as such, and the irrelevant or uncontrolled use of the stronger contrasts — both of a tonal or a dissonantal type — which alteration makes possible.

Such caution, however, is in no sense a solution of the real problems at hand. It is the strongest possible conviction of the author that the latter — like all real problems — are to be solved only by seeing them through; by seeking order and coherence not as qualities which are easily achieved by falling back on the older terms, but rather — fortified by a solid knowledge of the resources which tradition offers — through following the newer implications to their inherent conclusions and seeking an order and coherence — if necessary, a new one — in terms of these.

For the present, the student is counseled to keep strictly within the tonal orbit defined by his immediate task, and — as always — to cultivate his powers of discrimination to the utmost.

Exercises

Outer voices given. Altered chords indicated by asterisks, chords of resolution by figures.

Andantino

(7)

Outer voices given, no chords indicated.

Andante

(2)

Moderato

(3)

Adagio

(4)

Un poco lento

(5)

Soprano voice, no chords indicated.

Andante

(4)

Allegro

(5)

Allegretto

(8)

Andante moderato

(9)

Allegro moderato

(10)

CHAPTER

THIRTEEN

Modulation (III)

1. CHORDAL AMBIGUITY

The discussion of alteration has shown that any chord, given the appropriate contexts, may be used in several senses which are far removed from each other. The sense of a chord may, in other words, be shifted not only by means of a change in degree (e.g., $C_I = F_V$) but through actual or implied enharmonic change (see Figs. 202–205). This makes it possible, as has already been pointed out (p. 345), to juxtapose keys hitherto only distantly related — or perhaps, rather, to condense involved harmonic processes into a much shorter space than is possible by other means.

Such juxtapositions may be used in the service of either tonicization or, when the rhythmic context allows the requisite amount of contrast, modulation. The harmony approaches the chord through one door, so to speak, and leaves it through another.

In this respect, chordal ambiguity is similar to other means of modulation; it differs, however, in that here it is not primarily the degree of the scale, but the intervallic sense of the chord itself, that is shifted.

2. THE DIMINISHED SEVENTH CHORD AND THE AUGMENTED TRIAD

Especially adapted for this purpose are chords possessing, through their enharmonic structure, two or more very definite harmonic directions.

Most obvious of these chords are the diminished seventh and the augmented triad, which, while possessing regular functions in the diatonic system (pp. 110, 164–165), possess at the same time a certain ambiguity, in that their intervals are all equal and that in this respect all inversions are identical in structure.

The diminished seventh chord, for instance, has the following possibilities among its simpler resolutions:

FIG. 206

each one of which can be applied to any degree of the diatonic scale; e.g., is I in C, v in F, vi in e, ♮II in b, etc.

It is by no means useless to consider some of the apparently far-fetched relationships as well as the simpler ones, e.g.:

FIG. 207

The enharmonic versions of the same chord

FIG. 208

a VII$_5^6$ f♯ VII$_3^4$ e♭ VII$_2$

etc.   etc.   etc.

may be resolved in similar fashion.

The augmented triad

FIG. 209

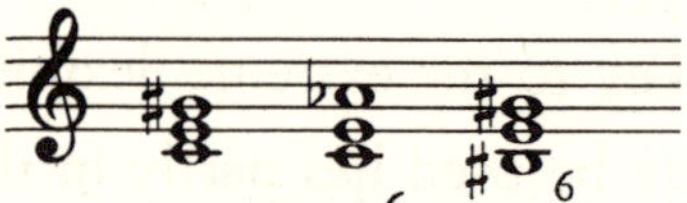

a III♯   f III^6♮   c♯III$^6_4$♯

can be treated in similar fashion, though its possibilities are more restricted, e.g.:

FIG. 210 *(a)*   *(b)*

can re-
solve to

The peculiar structure of these chords has as one of its results the fact that the number of possible chords in each type is limited by the number of semitones contained in the smallest interval of the chord in question. Since the diminished seventh, for instance, is built on superimposed minor thirds, chords may be built on each of any three successive semitones, e.g.:

FIG. 211

The chord on the next semitone being , it is, enharmonically considered, an inversion of the first chord in Figure 211, or, as far as relationships go, identical with it.

In like manner, there are four possibilities among augmented triads:

FIG. 212

The key to the extreme flexibility with which these chords may be used lies partly in the number of resolutions possible, but above all in the fact that the chords are both "neutral" and, apart from given contexts, devoid of inherent root implication. This latter attribute is due not only to the "neutrality" of the chords — that is, to the equality of the intervals — but, as may be seen in the case of other chords such as, for instance, the French sixth (p. 332), the fact that no two of the notes are, in any position, in the relationship of a perfect fifth.

For these reasons, any of the three diminished seventh chords, or any of the four augmented triads, may be introduced in any tonal context without disturbing or even influencing the tonal sense.

The following exercise, therefore, is not an exercise in modulation — which presents no problem whatever — but in resolution.

Exercise

Lead each of the three diminished seventh chords and each of the four augmented triads to a full cadence in each of the twenty-four keys, using as few chords as possible.

N.B. In using the augmented triad as an "altered chord," some difficulty will be noted in regard to doubling — a difficulty which obviously does not exist, in four-part writing, in the case of altered chords of four tones. Owing to the peculiar structure of the augmented triad it is clear that, out of context, any tone may equally well be doubled. In any given context, however, the tones which are treated as "altered" notes — i.e., those which move a semitone upward or downward — should preferably not be doubled. Each problem may be regarded as unique, however, and the student by this time should be in a position to evaluate it in its own terms, in relation to the sense of its musical design.

The exercise above, and the following group (modulations, p. 368), should be carried out, where possible, at the keyboard as well as on paper.

3. ENHARMONIC USE OF AUGMENTED SIXTH CHORDS, ETC.

The augmented sixth chords (pp. 331 ff.) may be used for enharmonic modulation in the same manner as those above. Examples:

FIG. 213

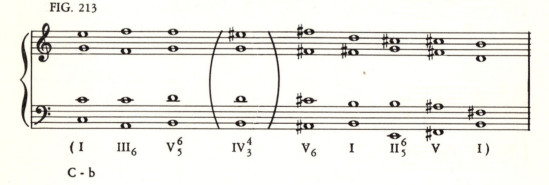

$$(I \quad III_6 \quad V^6_5 \quad IV^4_3 \quad V_6 \quad I \quad II^6_5 \quad V \quad I)$$

C - b

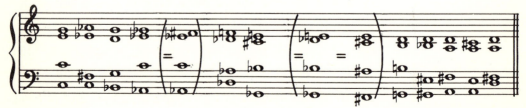

C - D

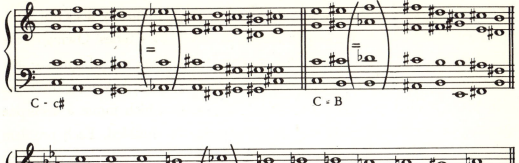

C - c♯   C = B

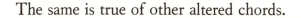

c - A

The same is true of other altered chords.

FIG. 214

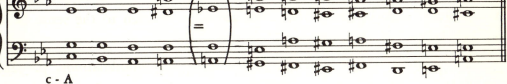

C - B   C - g♯

C - F♯

It will be found that altered chords which are enharmonically identical with unaltered root chords require
special attention if they are to be handled smoothly. Their
ambiguity is *specific* — that is, it depends on the substitution of one specific context for another — and not *general*, as in the case of the diminished seventh chord, whose

ambiguity is inherent in the structure of the chord. The only exception to this principle is the diminished triad, which can at any moment assume the role of an incomplete dominant seventh chord. The German sixth chord, on the other hand, is enharmonically identical with the dominant seventh chord, and therefore somewhat more restricted in its use than the French or the Italian sixth.

Exercises

Modulate, using the chord type indicated as pivot. The chords given may be used in any position or inversion, and may be transposed or enharmonically changed.

　　　1. Using 🎼, modulate as follows: Ab–f#; e–C#; F–b; c#–D; B–bb; g–Bb.

　　　2. Using 🎼, modulate as follows: d–G; E–Bb; a–g#; Gb–E; f–c#; C–A.

　　　3. Using 🎼, modulate as follows: Bb–C; f#–Eb; Db–d; ab–f#; G–F#; e–g#.

　　　4. Using 🎼, modulate as follows: c#–Eb; F#–a; d–g#; Eb–e; b–Bb; A–e.

　　　5. Using 🎼, modulate as follows: E–g; g#–D; Db–a; c#–c; F–d#; B–g.

4. JUXTAPOSITIONS OF KEYS

Changes of key of even a drastic nature are sometimes effected without any modulatory process whatever — that is to say, by simple juxtaposition. Obviously such juxtapositions are dependent on the rhythmic situation; that is, the keys in question must be embodied in separate rhythmic groups — motifs, phrases, sentences, or sections — and thus throw these groups into mutual relief.

Keys may be juxtaposed in this way as follows:

1. The cadential chord of one phrase may be utilized as a pivotal chord in respect to the opening of the following phrase. This does not by any means preclude the devices familiar under the heading of "alteration."

FIG. 215

A - F#

C - Eb

See page 198.

2. The second rhythmic group may be based on a sequential transposition of the first.

FIG. 216

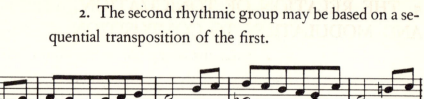

3. The phrases may be in such strong inherent contrast that a strong and even violent harmonic opposition merely underlines the general sense.

FIG. 217

5. THE RELATION OF TONICIZATION AND MODULATION TO COMPOSITION

Such considerations as the above lie on the border between strictly harmonic technique (in so far as such a thing exists at all) and the larger problems of composition. Two aspects of the problem deserve brief mention here.

First, *keys* are, in the sense of large musical structure, elaborated harmonies. In other words, the progression from C to G is different in degree, but not in essence, from the progression from I to V within the key of C major; the progression C–A♭ is identical, except in scale and intensity, with that of I–♭VI in C major, and so on.

This fact underlines the distinction between tonicization, which is a more or less wide inflection within the elaboration of a single key or progression, and modulation, which relates to the larger features of a composition.

Secondly, it may be seen from the above that not only the appropriateness of a given modulation, but the degree to which either the modulation itself, or the means by which it is accomplished, is really convincing, will depend on the place of the modulation in the tonal structure or flow of the work as a whole. In the final analysis — that is, on the largest scale — the concept of modulation merges with that of tonicization; the latter concept is useful chiefly in drawing attention to the distinction between harmonic detail and large harmonic design. In actual fact, the finest possible gradation exists, from, at one extreme, the slight inflection produced by a single secondary dominant or leading-tone chord, and, at the other extreme, the definitive modulation which introduces a large section of a string quartet or a symphony. The student must cultivate his awareness of these distinctions, not in verbal terms, which are inadequate and even, frequently, misleading, but through the practical cultivation of his musical ear — both in listening and doing.

Exercises

Outer voices given, no chords indicated.

Soprano voice, no chords indicated (1).

(4)

(5)

(6)

(7)

(8)

(9)

(10)

Complete the given phrase, modulating to the first key indicated; write a second phrase which modulates as further indicated.

(1)

→ B♭, *then to* D

→ f♯, *then to* F

→ G, *then to* B

→ D, *then to* b♭

→ B♭, *then to* F

→ C, *then to* D♭

→ A♭, *then to* G♭

Write a second "consequent" phrase to each of the following, modulating to the key indicated.

(3) → d♯

(4) → c♯

(5) → C♯

(6)

→ F

(7)

→ B

(8)

→ A

(9)

(10)

Soprano voice, no chords indicated (2).

On the model of the above exercises, complete the following. (Three phrases to each exercise.)

Construct a second phrase in each of the keys indicated, following one or the other of the principles illustrated on pages 369–370.

→ f minor, B major, E♭ major

→ F, a, c

CHAPTER

FOURTEEN

| Introduction to
Contemporary Harmonic
Practice |

1. INADEQUACY OF THEORY AS A GUIDE TO CONTEMPORARY PRACTICE

It is not the purpose of this final chapter to provide a key to contemporary harmonic technique or even to formulate its problems. It is even doubtful whether that can be done at the present time. Theory — at least on the level we have been considering — follows practice; the systematization of today's harmonic technique is still in the speculative stage. At best, in the author's opinion, it is possible to indicate some lines along which the processes of "harmonic thought" or, more correctly, "harmonic impulse" with which this book has dealt have developed further. What follows is not intended as a systematic or in any sense even a "true" indication of what has happened. The latter, in fact, would be both irrelevant and impossible. It is always possible, in technical matters, to observe effects, and to note the manner in which they may be considered as developments out of other effects;

but it is well to remember that such deductions are by their very nature oversimplified in the extreme. The musical ear — and, especially, the creative musical ear — is highly complex and infinitely subtle; it is composed of the finest of strands. As we approach contemporary musical developments we should clearly realize something which has always been true, but which the illusion of distance makes it possible all too frequently to ignore in connection with the music of the past: the fact that musical "technique" is not an isolated fact; that it is the product of many forces which have their ultimate roots not in the "materials" of music but in the human urges, the psychological and cultural patterns, which produce the materials.

The reason that the above paragraph occurs in a textbook on harmony is as follows: the closer the student approaches the music of his time, the more his relation to musical language is of necessity concrete and personal in a sense that is not the case in regard to materials which are "traditional." His attention will be captured more and more by specific instances which he will find increasingly difficult to generalize to any real technical advantage, however convenient such generalizations may be for purposes of communication.

The student must, then, study the materials of contemporary music above all in terms of individual works, and only to a far lesser extent in terms of "styles" or even of composers. If he is to become musically adult he will learn to make his own choices and evolve his own generalizations to the extent that he needs them. In this connection too the supremacy of the *ear* must be stressed;

he must make these choices and generalizations in terms of the ear — of the music to which he most truly responds (and if he is a composer, that which he wants to produce) — of the music which he learns to *possess* and the music which he is able to *make*. Abstract or a priori generalizations can only hinder and retard the student's musical development rather than help it, since they can have only the effect of keeping him away from the experiences on which his own choices and generalizations must be based.

The following general instances are given as indications of lines along which the student may proceed, with various instances in Chapters Seven to Thirteen as points of departure. No limits are given or indicated as to how far each line may be followed; and, in fact, they are in essence simply points of contact between what may be called traditional procedure, and the musical impulse, thought, and practice of today.

The latter must eventually, of course, be pursued in its integrity and on the basis of its own logic, which has developed out of the trains of thought indicated in this section along with many others. The following instances, therefore, are to be regarded as points of departure. If followed far enough, it will soon be found that they not only lead outside the purely harmonic sphere, but that they connect at certain points with each other, and that an adequate theoretical formulation of contemporary practice demands new terms and new conceptions well outside of the scope of this book.

What follows, therefore, aims simply to provide an introduction to contemporary practice. It should hardly be necessary to stress the fact that musical technique is not an end in itself, but only fulfills a function when it serves the purposes of musical imagination and expression; only when it does serve such purposes, in fact, does it pass beyond the mechanical and essentially primitive sphere, and achieve vital musical results.

This discussion will often presuppose harmony in more than four voices. At this point in the student's development this should cause him no problems, and further reference, therefore, will not be made to it.

2. SOME FURTHER PROCEDURES

Further diatonic procedures

1. A pedal point (see p. 199) may take the form of an "*ostinato*" — i.e., an insistent, repeated pattern which persists while the harmony moves:

FIG. 218

or it may be varied by ornamentation of varying degrees
of simplicity.

FIG. 219

2. A ninth, eleventh, or thirteenth chord (pp. 225–
228), or a derivation of such a chord, may be conceived
as consisting of superimposed chords, each of which develops as a distinct quasi-harmonic "plane."

FIG. 220

Care must be taken in such instances to avoid weakening
the sonority through excessive doubling, which produces
an effect analogous to that of the unison in two-voiced
counterpoint.

FIG. 221

* Note weakening of texture at this point.

But no rules can be made in this regard — the ear must decide, on the basis of the position, the instrumental or vocal medium, and the context.

As the musical vocabulary increases in complexity, it will be found that the diatonic and the chromatic categories tend to contrast more and more sharply with each other. Various conclusions may be drawn, and have been drawn, from this fact, ranging all the way from a possibly oversimplified conception, which regards the two categories as comparable respectively to those of consonance and dissonance, to an extreme dogmatism which regards them as mutually exclusive and even antagonistic. The present division has been adopted in the interests of expository convenience and should thus be interpreted, not in a theoretical, but rather in a purely practical, sense.

Further chromatic procedures

The techniques of alteration (Chapters Eight, Ten, and Twelve) and of enharmonic modulation (Chapter Thirteen) have the effect, not only of increasing the range of possible tonal relationships, but of allowing for their use in detail as well as in large design, for instance:

3. Harmonies remote from the key center may be tonicized, as well as those belonging to it:

FIG. 222

C I   B V$^4_3$ I$_6$ c♯ V   I$_6$ b♭ V$^4_3$ I I   C I

d♯ V   I   G♭ V   I

4. The process described under (2) (p. 387) may be extended to the chromatic category through the development of certain altered chords whose structure and usual resolution lend themselves to such a conception. The following trains of development should help to make this clear.

FIG. 223 (a)

(b)

*may be
expanded into*

*which may be fur-
ther elaborated, e.g.:*

(c)

or

(d)

5. Finally, alterations may, of course, proceed to other alterations.

FIG. 224

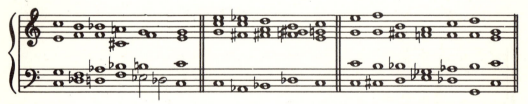

This is a procedure that leads, actually, as far as the ear will allow it to go, and which raises problems of which it is possible to give only the merest indication here. First, however, a few individual instances — on a relatively elementary level — may be briefly dealt with.

5*a.* Parallel seventh or ninth chords may be used diatonically:

FIG. 225

or chromatically:

FIG. 226

or in fact in any consistent linear pattern.

FIG. 227

5*b.* Tonally remote chords may be combined in sequential patterns, as for instance in the following examples from Wagner:

FIG. 228

Die Walküre

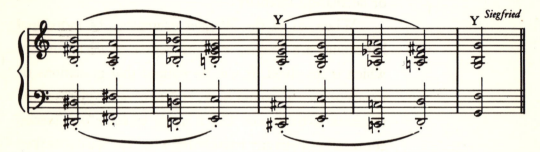

Siegfried

or, in a more developed sense, the following:

FIG. 229

Parsifal

The above examples bring to the fore the question of what may be called "sustained contrast." When highly contrasting materials are brought into juxtaposition, the "level of contrast" becomes an important element in respect to both musical logic and musical expression. The intensity of successive contrasts must either be maintained on a steady level, or be sensitively graded in increasing or decreasing intensity.

When, as in the Wagner examples, the individual harmonies are simple, it is the degree of *tonal* contrast which is involved. It will be noticed that gradations of tonal contrast at points X, Y, and Z serve the purposes of rhythmic articulation. But a single instance of lessened contrast between any two chords would seriously weaken the musical effect, e.g.:

FIG. 230

3. LINEAR IMPULSION AND DISSONANTAL TENSION

As has been pointed out (pp. 333–335, 344), the principle of alteration runs actually counter to that of root progression, in that it is based on the linear impulsion upward or downward of the single altered note and not on the relationship within a tonal framework (i.e., a key, or a quasi-key established through tonicization) of the various degrees. Every altered note, that is, is given the effect of a kind of secondary leading tone (see p. 248), tending either upward, like the leading tone proper, or downward, like the minor (Phrygian) second (p. 115) or even the minor sixth (p. 287). It differs from the latter, however, in that it does not necessarily tend toward — and therefore reinforce — the *root* of the chord which follows it, but may tend toward any of the tones of the latter, and in that, as in the augmented sixth but also very many other cases, a single chord may contain two, or three, or even more, altered notes. The horizontal pull of the voices is therefore intensified, and the relative force of the underlying root progressions — the specifically vertical or harmonic relationship — relatively weakened. Hence, in a series of consecutive chromatically altered chords — whether or not they are "altered chords" in the strict meaning of the term — the clear sense of root progression as such will tend to fall into the background even in cases where the root senses and even root relationships are clear. In more radical cases, this sense of root progression will disappear completely, and give way to the chromatic impulse of the alterations, and, in a larger sense, to the polyphonic impulse which these altered notes set in motion.

The examples from Wagner on page 392 can be cited in clarification of this point. All three examples can certainly be analyzed in terms of root progression. The terms used will register fleeting tonal impressions, but these will be at best insufficient in giving a clear picture of the musical sense — i.e., the movement — of the passages in question, and at worst will be ambiguous.

FIG. 231

One may ask, in the context above, what is the actual relation of the tonalities indicated — i.e., b♭ is not VII of b, b is not ♮II of b♭, etc.

Actually, the figuration is quite meaningless, since it is necessarily in terms of keys which exist at best only in theory, for the eye alone; for the harmonies are entirely transitional, as the reduction below shows; there is at no time a point of rest, a goal in either a rhythmic or harmonic sense, until the final chord of Figure 231 — a chord already present in the first measure.

FIG. 232

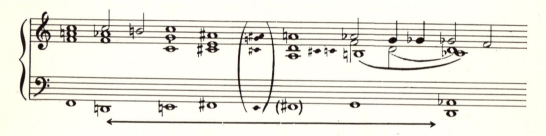

In order to account adequately for the sense of the passages in question (p. 392), one must recognize two factors other than that of root progression as conditioning the choice of specific harmonies: (1) the linear or melodic design, and relative movement, of the outer voices, including the quasi-cadential articulations of that movement, and (2) what has been described (p. 393) as the "level of contrast."

If this is true in regard to the above passages, it becomes far more true in the case of chords of more complex structure. In progressions formed of successive chords of this type, the motivating design will be shifted away to an even greater extent from the pull of tonality and of key relationships. The sustained contrast, so important in the Wagner examples, will be supplemented, enhanced, and even superseded by the tension inherent in dissonance — dissonance sustained or graded in the same way as the contrasts which are so essential in the Wagner examples and progressions of a similar nature.

By "*dissonantal tension*" is meant the specific *quantity* of dissonance — quantity being the category under which, for instance, the minor second and major seventh are often classified as "more dissonant" than the major second and the minor seventh. Thus the dissonantal tension is noticeably higher in chord (a) than in chord (b) of Figure 233, and in both (a) and (b) it is higher than in chord (c).

FIG. 233

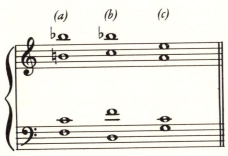

The principle involved at this point — that of sustaining the dissonantal tension — is analogous, on a quite different scale, to that which, in strict counterpoint, forbids unisons in two-voiced, and open fifths in three-voiced, writing.

The analogy between this principle and that described on page 393 derives from the fact that when two successive chords are in strong tonal contrast to each other, each is dissonant in terms of the other, as the following examples show; and from the fact that anything which underlines that contrast — such as a change of position — accentuates this quasi-dissonantal or pseudo-dissonantal effect.

FIG. 234

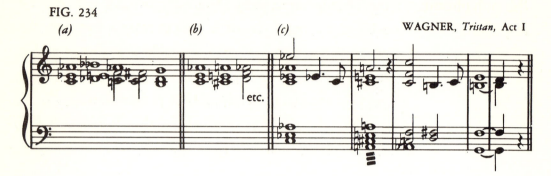

WAGNER, *Tristan*, Act I

WAGNER, *Tristan*, Act II

STRAUSS, *Elektra*

4. TECHNICAL PROBLEMS OF TODAY

The student who makes extended and radical use of "altered" chords will, for the above reasons, inevitably find himself thinking in terms of voice progression, that

Supremacy of the polyphonic impulse

is to say, in polyphonic terms; and the sonorities which he achieves will result from the shifting of voices to at least as great a degree as from the specific character of the chords themselves. For only in this way can he achieve a connection or a logical pattern between the chords which is in any way comparable to that provided by the now (for reasons mentioned above, pp. 333, 344, 393) superseded principle of root progression.

It is fairly easy to demonstrate this. If a passage like the following

FIG. 235

is developed further, with care to maintain a consistent level of tension, it will be perceived that the impulsion which carries it along is contrapuntal; in other words, that as one proceeds from one chord or sonority to another, it is the leading of the voices — above all the outer ones — which determines the choice of chords. It is however a general constancy in the degree of dissonantal tension — which in this example increases in power from the first to the fifth chord — which gives the voices their impulsive power.

Other results of such a procedure may be mentioned. First of all, by the time the use of the process of alteration has led this far, the term "alteration" itself has long since ceased to have any meaning. The term implies the continued importance of "root progression" as a determining factor; otherwise, what is it that is being "altered"? The term may still be used, as it is used here, because the purposes of this book are best served by describing procedures for as long as possible in terms of their apparent technical origin, especially when satisfactory new terms have not yet been invented for them. But it would be false to think of the tones of a chord as "alterations" when there is no indication of what is "altered."

The real point is that the "chord" as a valid concept, as an entity, has, in this type of progression, once more ceased to exist, much as it may be said not to have existed in the pretonal technique. What prevails is a certain sonorous quality which results from, and is incidental to, the interplay of voices which maintain a certain constancy of total dissonance among themselves. One result, in terms of this, is that there are no "stable" tones; and, since this is the case, the questions of doubling tones, and of repeating them, after digression, at too close intervals of time, become of the greatest importance. In specific if somewhat oversimplified terms: when every tone is a potential "alteration" and thus has a "tendency" (i.e., as a "leading tone," ascending or descending as described on page 394), the question of doubling becomes problematical, and the too close repetition of any note, especially in one or the other of the outer voices, may easily threaten the flexibility of the movement by creating a static element where it is not wanted.

The following two figures may be regarded as illustrations of this point:

FIG. 236
(Lento)

The repetition of C♯ in the lowest voice (at "X," Fig. 236) gives this tone too much emphasis, producing a less fluid effect. It could be corrected by using C♮ in the first instance.

FIG. 237

Here the repetition of F (at "X," Fig. 237) produces a similar effect. An F♯ at "a" and a G♯ at "b" would remedy the situation.

Refinement of the concept of "dissonance"

It is hardly necessary to point out that the term "dissonance" has also become quite inadequate long before this point. This is not a question of the disappearance of distinctions, but of their refinement. The maintenance of two categories ("consonance" and "dissonance") has lost its meaning, not in order to abolish all categories, but in order to recognize the subtlest shades of distinction, and to reformulate musical theory accordingly. Dissonantal tension, as has already been pointed out (p. 397), is a matter, not only of intervals used, but of context; this appears on the most elementary level, in fact, in the contrasting conception of the minor third and the augmented second, etc.

Various efforts have been made already toward formulating, in a reasonably clear and exact manner, principles by which the degree of dissonantal tension can be measured. In the author's opinion, such efforts belong still in the realm of speculative theory, and therefore are outside the limits of this book. It is doubtful, in fact, whether such a formulation can ever be made in a completely convincing manner, owing to the importance of individual contexts; and it is preferable in any case that the student learn through his own constant experience and observation. As always, he should ceaselessly cultivate his ear, through careful listening, through "trial and error," and also, to a very large degree, through self-reliance. He should realize that, on these terms, his ear will be infallible, and should simply strive with the utmost energy to meet the terms.

Problem of the cadence

The student will not have occupied himself very long with the subject of these final paragraphs before finding himself confronted by the very crucial problem of the cadence. He will perhaps feel already, in some of the music of the late nineteenth and early twentieth centuries (e.g., Strauss, especially *Salome* and *Elektra*), a somewhat problematical discrepancy in dissonantal tension between certain highly charged progressions and the cadences to which they resolve. The problem is, to be sure, not merely that of this constantly recurring discrepancy, but is intimately bound up with the problem of tonality itself (pp. 404–409).

His efforts to solve the problem of the cadence will necessarily be individual, in the opinion of the author, since no really inclusive (and therefore no completely satisfying) theoretical formulation of contemporary harmonic problems has yet appeared. The composers of today are still furnishing the data, so to speak, on which such formulations must necessarily be based.

What the composer of today must do, therefore, is to cultivate as clear a sense as possible for musical articulation as such. His phrases, periods, and sections must really take shape, and must come to satisfying closes, partly as a result of satisfactory movement toward the closes. He can achieve this only if his harmonic and rhythmic conception is clear — it is not essential that he be able to "explain" it in words, technical or otherwise. Conscious theories will not help him, except in so far as they consist in observation after the fact. He must in other words cultivate a *feeling* for articulation, and then achieve it in his own terms.

Essentially this is, of course, what composers have always done; it is easy to overestimate the extent to which composers have relied on generalizations. If one studies the problem of articulation, as composers have solved it at all times, it can be seen very easily how original each successive generation of composers has been in this respect. This can be observed not only in the work of composers of successive generations, but in successive phases of the work of a single composer. If one compares, for instance, the two volumes of Bach's *Well-Tempered Clavier*, Beethoven's Op. 57 or Op. 59 with his Op. 106 or Op. 131, *Lohengrin* with *Parsifal*, or *Rigoletto* with *Falstaff*, one can easily see how independent the composers have been in these matters, and how little generalizations have to do with the real problem in its complete aspect, which is rhythmic and melodic as well as harmonic. It is never a question of applying a formula, but of solving a problem, in each case, in accordance with the composer's ideas and the technical necessities which these ideas create.

Problem of tonality

The problem of tonality also belongs in the realm of speculative theory, and, as the author has already stated (p. 29), he believes that it will be some time before the principles of tonality have been adequately reformulated in order to cover the music of the present day. Several points may and should be borne in mind, however.

First of all, this problem is not one which has arisen in the music of any single group of composers; rather, it has arisen in contemporary music as a whole; the problem is one whose origins reach back quite palpably into the music of the mid-nineteenth century, and very possibly are inherent in the development of tonality itself. It should be clear, for instance, that, even for those composers who are farthest from the radically chromatic idiom to which the term "atonal" is most generally applied, "tonality" is something quite different from the "tonality" of the last three hundred years. It is different in its motivations, in its principles of procedure, and in its effects. It is so because it represents a deliberate *selection* of some of the available materials, and an equally deliberate *exclusion* of others. In this manner it differs from the earlier, expansive tonality, which was based on the use, by composers of each successive generation, of all materials bequeathed to them by their predecessors, and the gradual expansion of harmonic resources. The "tonal" composers of today are limited, not so much by the materials and the principles they have inherited from their predecessors, as by restrictions which they have imposed on themselves. This is said not by way of objection, but rather to point out that their "tonality," like the so-called "atonality" to which they are opposed, is something new, to which traditional principles no longer apply.

New formulations, however, will not be valid or convincing unless they are descriptions of musical facts rather than elaborations of aesthetic attitudes. They must be essentially nondogmatic formulations which, like the principles of tonality at the time of their first discovery, seek to include, in the most complete manner, all of the data available. They must include the past, in much the same way that the principle of tonality is not irreconcilable with "modality," but brings to the latter, as it were, a new dimension. They must include, in the same manner, all that is vital in the various tendencies of today; and for this reason it may well be that they can come only as a result of the achievement of such a synthesis, first of all, by the creative imagination of composers in their works.

What is needed is a new and far more inclusive description of the various relationships between tones, and of the means by which the "musical ear" discriminates, selects, and arranges these relationships — the basis, that is, on which the ear orients itself, and on which the composers of today organize musical sound. The twelve-tone system, for example, provides a possible answer to one aspect of this question, by offering a basis of organization through an ordered selection of relationships. It deserves the most serious study from this point of view; the heat of controversy has obscured the real nature of the system, of the function which it performs, and of the relationship of the composer to it. Like any other technique — like the matters with which the present volume deals — it demands mastery, and the transition from calculation to spontaneity can come only as mastery is achieved: that is in fact the whole object of study.

The twelve-tone technique, however, does not provide the answer to the question of how the ear perceives, co-ordinates, and synthesizes the relationships involved, nor does it attempt to do so. Its nature is essentially practical; and when it is used by composers of imagination who have really mastered it, the experienced listener will inevitably be aware of what may be called "tonal areas" or "tonal centers." But in no real sense are these matters definable in the older terms. For instance, in listening to the first movement of Schönberg's *Fourth Quartet* (Op. 37), he will receive sensations which will suggest to him the key of D, even specifically d minor; but if he tries to analyze these sensations in terms of this key in any known or knowable form, he will find himself at a loss; and if he tries to formulate his tonal impressions in any other known technical terms, he will find that he can adduce only the most fragmentary and hopelessly inadequate bits of evidence.

Such quasi-tonal sensations are simply evidence that his ear has grasped the relationships between the tones, and has absorbed and ordered them. It is a mistake to regard such sensations as connected exclusively with the tonal system as such. The intervals, and their effects, remain precisely the same; two tones a fifth apart still produce the effect of the fifth, and, in whatever degree the context permits, will convey a sensation similar to that of a root and its fifth, or of a tonic and its dominant. A rising interval of a semitone will produce somewhat the effect of a "leading tone," principal or secondary, and so on. Problems have arisen, not because these basic relationships have in any way changed in their inherent sense, but because the music of the late nineteenth and the twentieth centuries has built them into more complex, or at least hitherto unfamiliar, patterns. The more complex a combination of tones is, the more manifold are the tensions which it contains, and the more difficult it is to define in any fixed manner the functions of its various tones (cf. Chapter Thirteen). Such a combination or complex is, from the strictly tonal point of view, overcharged — there is an oversaturation of tonal impulse. Just as this oversaturation has the effect of superseding the principle of root progression, and gives rise to a new polyphony (pp. 399 ff.), so it leads beyond tonality as hitherto conceived.

In superseding the principle of root progression it does not, of course, abolish either the "vertical" element in music, or the possibility of vertical relationships analogous to root relationships between harmonies. Mention has been made, for instance, of "tonal areas" perceived in so-called "atonal" music (p. 406). The attentive ear is aware not only of such "tonal areas" but of contrasting ones. If, however, such contrasts — akin in principle to contrasts of key in "tonal" music — are to be given precise technical definition, the areas themselves must be defined, in terms of the elements which produce them, the role which each of the twelve tones plays in setting them up, and the means by which the sense of the tonal area is shifted or destroyed.

It ought to be clear from the above paragraphs that the author regards the term "atonality" as at best a temporary slogan of doubtful usefulness. If it is taken literally in the sense of its derivation, it implies music in which the tones have no relationship to each other — an impossibility; and it is in any case an evasion of the real issue, which is that of what is actually heard in music. It is also a negative term, which defines nothing and describes nothing; it is in fact quite meaningless, since there is no real line of demarcation between the "tonal" and the "atonal" and no means by which "atonality" could be demonstrated except in the most arbitrary manner. The problem, once more, is that of adequately redefining the relationships between tones, in the light of the music — all of the music — of the present day, and of formulat-

ing new tonal principles which will be adequate to that
music and useful to the future student. That is the task,
and one of the first order, for the future musical theorist.

Exercises

The following exercises are suggested as providing a practical introduction to the problems discussed in this final chapter. They constitute an introduction to processes of thought and not conclusions of such processes; they are experimental in character. The student may carry them as far as he wishes, but he should try to sense the point at which they have been carried far enough, and to arrive at a conclusion that will be reasonably convincing, with the means thus far at his disposal.

Develop the following along the lines indicated on page 386.

Develop along the lines indicated on pages 387 and 389–390.

Allegro

(2)

Andante

(3)

Moderato

(4)

Continue and develop.

(1)

(2)

(3)

(4)

(5)

(6)

(7)

Appendixes

APPENDIX A

References to musical works

The following list of references is to be regarded as supplemental to the text, and not as an exhaustive list of instances. The student should form the habits, as early as possible, of observation and analysis, and should therefore learn to seek, as well as to recognize, as many and as varied examples as possible of the various technical points as they occur. The effort has therefore been made, in this appendix, to provide clear instances of such points as most need illustration, but to avoid burdening the student by citing examples he can easily find for himself.

Chapter Four

Root Relationships (pp. 72–77)

RELATIONSHIP OF THE FIFTH

Haydn, *Quartet in D Major*, Op. 76, No. 5, Finale, mm. 1–6 (v–1).

Beethoven, *Piano Sonata*, Op. 57, slow movement, mm. 1–2 (1–IV–1).

Brahms, *Rhapsody*, Op. 119, No. 4, mm. 1–4.

RELATIONSHIP OF THE THIRD

Wagner, *Siegfried*, Act III, Scene III (p. 297 of Schirmer's edition), Brünnhilde's Awakening, "*Heil Dir, Sonne*" (III–1).

Wagner, *Lohengrin*, Prelude, mm. 5–6 (1–VI–1).

Wagner, *Parsifal*, Prelude, mm. 39–41 (1–VI–IV–II–(v)–1).

RELATIONSHIP OF THE SECOND

Wagner, *Siegfried*, Act III, Scene III,

Brünnhilde's words, "*Heil Dir, Licht*" (III–11).

Debussy, *Pelleas et Melisande*, mm. 1–4 (I–VII twice repeated).

Berlioz, *Requiem*, Agnus Dei, mm. 1–2.

Harmonic Movement (pp. 77–82)

Compare Haydn, *Quartet in D Major*, Op. 76, No. 5, Finale, with Tchaikovsky, *Symphony No. 4*, Scherzo (pizzicato).

Compare Schubert, *Moment Musical*, Op. 94, No. 5, with Brahms, *Rhapsody*, Op. 119, No. 4.

EVENNESS OF TEXTURE, CONTINUITY OF MOVEMENT (p. 80)

Bach, Gigue from *French Suite No. 2*, c minor.

CUMULATIVE HARMONIC MOVEMENT

Beethoven, *Piano Sonata*, Op. 2, No. 2, Largo, mm. 1–19.

The Cadence (pp. 85–87)

PLAGAL CADENCE

Chopin, *Étude*, Op. 10, No. 12, last two measures.

Brahms, *Symphony No. 1*, last eleven measures.

Beethoven, *Missa Solemnis*, Credo, last four measures.

DECEPTIVE CADENCE

Mozart, *Die Zauberflöte*, No. 9, March of the Priests, mm. 23–24, 25–26.

Wagner, *Tristan und Isolde*, Prelude, mm. 16–17.

Beethoven, *Piano Sonata*, Op. 7, Largo, mm. 19–20.

Bach, *Prelude No. 8 in E♭ Minor* (*Well-Tempered Clavier*, Book I), mm. 28–29.

Mozart, *Piano Concerto in E♭ Major* (K. 482), slow movement, mm. 27–28.

HALF CADENCE

Beethoven, *Piano Sonata*, Op. 14, No. 2, Andante, mm. 2, 4.

Brahms, *Violin Concerto*, first movement, m. 7.

Mozart, *Piano Concerto in B♭ Major* (K. 595), slow movement, m. 4.

Expressive Accentuation (pp. 89–92)

Beethoven, *Piano Sonata*, Op. 2, No. 2, Largo, mm. 6, 18.

Beethoven, *Leonore Overture No. 3*, Allegro, m. 2.

Beethoven, *Symphony No. 3*, Marcia Funebre, m. 6.

SYNCOPATION IN TRIPLE TIME

Beethoven, *Piano Sonata*, Op. 2, No. 2, Largo, mm. 16–17.

Beethoven, *Sonata for Violoncello and Piano*, Op. 102, No. 2, Finale (fugue), mm. 2–3 of subject.

Beethoven, *Symphony No. 3*, first movement, mm. 25–26, 29–34, 53–54, 119–121, 128–131.

SYNCOPATION IN DUPLE AND QUADRUPLE TIME

Beethoven, *Sonata for Violoncello and Piano*, Op. 102, No. 2, first movement, mm. 1, 2.

Beethoven, *Leonore Overture No. 3*, mm. 160–179.

See also Brahms, *Symphony No. 2*, Allegretto grazioso, mm. 1, 2.

See also Beethoven, *Quartet*, Op. 130, second movement (presto), mm. 17–22.

Chapter Six

Seventh Chords in Succession (p. 174)

Brahms, *Sonata for Clarinet and Piano*, Op. 120, No. 1, second movement, mm. 1–4 (VI₇–II₇–V₇–I).

Beethoven, *Piano Sonata*, Op. 2, No. 1, mm. 11–14.

See also Bach, *Prelude No. 3 in C♯ Major* (*Well-Tempered Clavier*, Book II), mm. 9–11, 12–13, 16–17.

late nineteenth and early twentieth centuries, and the available resources are so unlimited, that no attempt is made here to illustrate in detail the principles of modulation through enharmonic change. A few typical instances, beginning with the simplest, are cited below, together with some which must be considered outstanding as strokes of genius; for the rest, the student will find himself at no loss if he investigates the scores of Wagner, Liszt, Franck, Bruckner, Reger, etc.

Mozart, *Don Giovanni*, No. 20, Sextet, m. 27 (entrance of Donna Anna and Don Ottavio); Beethoven, *Symphony No. 4*, first movement, mm. 304–305; Chopin, *Polonaise in C Minor*, Op. 40, No. 2, mm. 73–75. (This is not strictly a modulation, but well illustrates the principle involved and is cited here for that reason.)

Also, Beethoven, *Piano Sonata*, Op. 106, first movement, after the double bar, mm. 96–108. (The disputed A-sharp at the end of this passage seems to this writer authentic beyond all doubt, in spite of the evidence cited by Schenker and others against it.

The evidence proves, certainly, that Beethoven at one time intended to write A-natural; it is nevertheless true that Beethoven on many occasions made changes in works even after they had passed well beyond the stage of sketches. If the A-sharp is altered to A-natural, the passage seems to this writer, as it has seemed to many musicians, unique among Beethoven's mature works for the weakness of the return of the theme; the effect of A-sharp is immeasurably stronger. Since it is, after all, the A-sharp, occurring eight times in succession, which has been left unaltered both in the manuscript and in the first edition, the present writer feels more than justified in accepting the A-sharp as representing Beethoven's final version.

An oversight seems nearly out of the question here, not only because the tone in question has been left eight times unaltered, but because the corresponding note in each of the previous figures (G-natural, G-sharp) has been altered. It should be pointed out, too, that the notation A-sharp — F-natural, illogical as it has seemed to some commentators, nevertheless perfectly underlines the formal situation. The logical place for the enhar-

monic change from A-sharp to B-flat is precisely where it occurs, at the opening of the recapitulation; an E-sharp, however, would be completely senseless, since the F is the dominant preparation for the B-flat, and the pivotal tone in the whole process. This should be clear if, on the basis of the A-sharp, one tries to work out a more satisfactory notation for the passage as a whole. In the opinion of the writer, and on the basis of whatever objectivity he is able to muster, this cannot be done.

It must be admitted, no doubt, that there is no completely convincing "objective" method of settling this question on the basis of evidence at hand. All composers of all periods have occasionally overlooked accidentals, and Beethoven not less than others. This should be recognized by both sides of the controversy, which will doubtless continue to rage, and to be settled by individual musicians with temperament and instinct as the decisive factors here, as they must ultimately be in all artistic matters where value judgments are involved.)

Also, Beethoven, *Variations on a Theme by Diabelli*, variation xxxii, the last six measures (poco adagio); Franck, *Symphony in D Minor*, first movement, mm. 472–473 (cited as an example of the pitfalls into which the facility of this type of modulation can lead even a gifted and able composer).

Juxtapositions of Keys (pp. 368–370)

Beethoven, *Symphony No. 6*, third movement, mm. 1–16.

Beethoven, *Piano Sonata*, Op. 110, allegro molto, mm. 1–8.

Beethoven, *Bagatelle in F Major*, Op. 33, No. 3, mm. 1–8.

Beethoven, *Bagatelle in B Minor*, Op. 126, No. 4, mm. 1–8.

Chapter Fourteen

No specific references are given for this chapter. The matters there discussed cover a broad field of musical development which has been taking place over the last hundred years, and the specific instances discussed are merely illustrations of certain easily identifiable lines along which that development has proceeded. It is absolutely imperative, therefore, that, apart from certain specific technical exercises, to which the chapter may be considered an introduction, the student should familiarize himself with the music of the whole period in as thorough and also as comprehensive a manner as possible; he should also familiarize himself with the currents of musical thought which this music represents. In particular, the mature music of Schönberg, Stravinsky, and Bartok should be studied with the utmost attention; the student should try, seriously and without *parti pris*, to understand the evolution of the modes of thought of these composers. Aural mastery, rather than aesthetic evaluation, should be the student's primary goal, since such evaluation cannot be achieved in any convincing manner except on a basis of real intimacy with the music itself.

For special study, therefore, at least a selection from the following works is recommended — it being understood, first, that the list is necessarily incomplete; and, secondly, that it assumes some real acquaintance with the music which constitutes its immediate background: Mahler, Debussy, Strauss, Ravel, etc.

Schönberg: *Pierrot Lunaire*; piano pieces (Op. 11, Op. 19, Op. 23, Op. 33); *Variations for Orchestra* (Op. 31); *Quartet No. 3*; *Quartet No. 4*; *Concerto for Violin and Orchestra*; *Concerto for Piano and Orchestra*.

Stravinsky: *Le Sacre du Printemps*; *Les Noces*; *Octuor for Wind Instruments*; *Symphonie de Psaumes*; *Orpheus*; *Symphony in Three Movements*.

Bartok: *Quartets* (Nos. 2, 4, 5, 6); *Music for Strings, Celesta, and Percussion*; *Sonata for Two Pianos and Percussion*.

APPENDIX B

Sample solutions to Exercises

The following are to be considered, not as examples of what is expected of the student, but rather as indications of the type of goal toward which he may strive. He will find it helpful to analyze each solution carefully, attempting first to "understand" aurally, and then if possible to formulate for himself, in technical terms, the reasons for each step taken.

(Allegro moderato (♩ =160))

Page 69, No. 10

Page 102, No. 9

Andante moderato (♪ =112)

Page 116, No. 6

Page 118, No. 9

Andante (♩=60) Page 123, No. 11

Lento (♩=72) Page 126, No. 12

Presto (♪.=176)   Page 143, No. 7

Moderato (♩ =88)   Page 184, No. 3

Page 222, No. 7

Andantino (♩ =126)

Allegro (♩ = 138)

Page 236, No. 2

Andante tranquillo (♪ =116)

Page 241, No. 7

Allegretto   (♪ =96)   Page 264, No. 2

Lento (♩ = 50) Page 265, No. 6

Andante (♪ =112)   Page 305, No. 8

Allegretto (♩ =92)

Page 307, No. 6

Adagio (♩ =69)

Page 379, No. 10

Tempo di mazurka (♩ =100)

Page 382, No. 6

Index

* Page references in italics indicate descriptions of the use of chords in four-voiced harmony exercises. Alterations are marked as in the keys without sharps or flats — i.e., C major and a minor.